"Congress shall make no law ... abridging the freedom of speech, or of the press."

First Amendment to the US Constitution

The basic foundation of our democracy is the First Amendment guarantee of freedom of expression. The Opposing Viewpoints series is dedicated to the concept of this basic freedom and the idea that it is more important to practice it than to enshrine it.

OPPOSING
VIEWPOINTS®
SERIES

Peoples on the Move: The Immigration Crisis

Lita Sorensen, Book Editor

GREENHAVEN
PUBLISHING

Published in 2023 by Greenhaven Publishing, LLC
29 East 21st Street
New York, NY 10010

Library of Congress Cataloging-in-Publication Data

Names: Sorensen, Lita, editor.
Title: Peoples on the move : the immigration crisis / Lita Sorensen, book
    editor.
Description: First edition. | New York : Greenhaven Publishing, 2023. |
    Series: Opposing viewpoints | Includes bibliographical references and
    index. | Audience: Ages: 15 | Audience: Grades: 10–12 | Summary:
    "Anthology of essays written from diverse perspectives that examine the
    current immigration crisis"— Provided by publisher.
Identifiers: LCCN 2021059677 | ISBN 9781534508750 (library binding) | ISBN
    9781534508743 (paperback)
Subjects: LCSH: Emigration and immigration law—United States—Juvenile
    literature. | Immigrants—United States—Juvenile literature. |
    Refugees—United States—Juvenile literature. | United
    States—Emigration and immigration—Government policy—Juvenile
    literature.
Classification: LCC JV6483 .P445 2023 | DDC 325.73—dc23/eng/20220105
LC record available at https://lccn.loc.gov/2021059677

Manufactured in the United States of America

Website: http://greenhavenpublishing.com

Contents

Chapter 1: What Defines an Immigration Crisis?

Chapter 2: Is the Immigration Crisis Actually Several Different Crises?

Chapter 3: What Humanitarian Problems Does the Immigration Crisis Create?

Chapter 4: What Is the Future of Immigration Policy?

The Importance of Opposing Viewpoints

Perhaps every generation experiences a period in time in which the populace seems especially polarized, starkly divided on the important issues of the day and gravitating toward the far ends of the political spectrum and away from a consensus-facilitating middle ground. The world that today's students are growing up in and that they will soon enter as active and engaged citizens is deeply fragmented in just this way. Issues relating to terrorism, immigration, women's rights, minority rights, race relations, health care, taxation, wealth and poverty, the environment, policing, military intervention, the proper role of government—in some ways, perennial issues that are freshly and uniquely urgent and vital with each new generation—are currently roiling the world.

If we are to foster a knowledgeable, responsible, active, and engaged citizenry among today's youth, we must provide them with the intellectual, interpretive, and critical-thinking tools and experience necessary to make sense of the world around them and of the all-important debates and arguments that inform it. After all, the outcome of these debates will in large measure determine the future course, prospects, and outcomes of the world and its peoples, particularly its youth. If they are to become successful members of society and productive and informed citizens, students need to learn how to evaluate the strengths and weaknesses of someone else's arguments, how to sift fact from opinion and fallacy, and how to test the relative merits and validity of their own opinions against the known facts and the best possible available information. The landmark series Opposing Viewpoints has been providing students with just such critical-thinking skills and exposure to the debates surrounding society's most urgent contemporary issues for many years, and it continues to serve this essential role with undiminished commitment, care, and rigor.

The key to the series's success in achieving its goal of sharpening students' critical-thinking and analytic skills resides in its title—

Opposing Viewpoints. In every intriguing, compelling, and engaging volume of this series, readers are presented with the widest possible spectrum of distinct viewpoints, expert opinions, and informed argumentation and commentary, supplied by some of today's leading academics, thinkers, analysts, politicians, policy makers, economists, activists, change agents, and advocates. Every opinion and argument anthologized here is presented objectively and accorded respect. There is no editorializing in any introductory text or in the arrangement and order of the pieces. No piece is included as a "straw man," an easy ideological target for cheap point-scoring. As wide and inclusive a range of viewpoints as possible is offered, with no privileging of one particular political ideology or cultural perspective over another. It is left to each individual reader to evaluate the relative merits of each argument— as he or she sees it, and with the use of ever-growing critical-thinking skills—and grapple with his or her own assumptions, beliefs, and perspectives to determine how convincing or successful any given argument is and how the reader's own stance on the issue may be modified or altered in response to it.

This process is facilitated and supported by volume, chapter, and selection introductions that provide readers with the essential context they need to begin engaging with the spotlighted issues, with the debates surrounding them, and with their own perhaps shifting or nascent opinions on them. In addition, guided reading and discussion questions encourage readers to determine the authors' point of view and purpose, interrogate and analyze the various arguments and their rhetoric and structure, evaluate the arguments' strengths and weaknesses, test their claims against available facts and evidence, judge the validity of the reasoning, and bring into clearer, sharper focus the reader's own beliefs and conclusions and how they may differ from or align with those in the collection or those of their classmates.

Research has shown that reading comprehension skills improve dramatically when students are provided with compelling, intriguing, and relevant "discussable" texts. The subject matter of these collections could not be more compelling, intriguing, or urgently relevant to today's students and the world they are poised to inherit. The anthologized articles and the reading and discussion questions that are included with them also provide the basis for stimulating, lively, and passionate classroom debates. Students who are compelled to anticipate objections to their own argument and identify the flaws in those of an opponent read more carefully, think more critically, and steep themselves in relevant context, facts, and information more thoroughly. In short, using discussable text of the kind provided by every single volume in the Opposing Viewpoints series encourages close reading, facilitates reading comprehension, fosters research, strengthens critical thinking, and greatly enlivens and energizes classroom discussion and participation. The entire learning process is deepened, extended, and strengthened.

For all of these reasons, Opposing Viewpoints continues to be exactly the right resource at exactly the right time—when we most need to provide readers with the critical-thinking tools and skills that will not only serve them well in school but also in their careers and their daily lives as decision-making family members, community members, and citizens. This series encourages respectful engagement with and analysis of opposing viewpoints and fosters a resulting increase in the strength and rigor of one's own opinions and stances. As such, it helps make readers "future ready," and that readiness will pay rich dividends for the readers themselves, for the citizenry, for our society, and for the world at large.

Introduction

"The size and scope of the global forced migration crisis are unprecedented. …This global crisis already poses serious challenges to economic growth and risks to stability and national security, as well as an enormous human toll affecting tens of millions of people."

—*Center for Strategic and International Studies*

The issues surrounding migration and the flow of peoples across the globe are complex and varied. Today, more people than ever before reside in countries other than those in which they were born. In 2019, an estimated 272 million immigrants were on the move, 51 million more than in 2010. Migrants of various types, including refugees, asylum seekers, those seeking employment, and those seeking a better life for themselves have compelled journalists, governments, and scholars to ask questions about these migrants, the places they leave, and their destination countries.

Migration is often classed in terms of a push-pull dynamic, with voluntary migration and forced migration alike the result of economic, political, and social factors. Involuntary migrants are often termed refugees or asylum seekers and are fleeing political conflict like genocide or war. Climate refugees, those seeking to relocate due to natural disasters, also fall into this group. Voluntary migration is often classed as economic or labor migration, with individuals and families looking for better jobs and lifestyles.

Voluntary migration stresses the idea of the free will of individuals and families to leave their countries of origin. Push factors might include negative aspects of their home country, such as lack of economic opportunity or relative development (examples might be poor water, air quality, or sanitation). There may also be significant perceived "pull" factors, such as better paying work, which has historically been the case with immigrants from Mexico and other South American countries crossing the border into the United States.

Forced migration is a hotly debated topic for political and sociological reasons. *Forced Migration Review*, a scientific journal devoted to such study, says forced migration refers to the movement of refugees and internally displaced people (in other words, displaced by conflict) in addition to those displaced by disasters, famine, or man-made nuclear or chemical threats. The events force people to leave, often in fear for their lives. These immigrants often don't want to leave their beloved homelands and are displaced in camps, seeking asylum in other countries often halfway around the globe.

Research suggests that immigration of all sorts can be beneficial to both countries of origin and the destination countries. Some studies show that the influx of low-skilled workers does affect native populations of the same skill level in a negative way. Other research offers the idea that the elimination of controls on immigration altogether would grossly impact worldwide production, with gains estimating from 67 percent to 147 percent increase and would be extremely effective in eliminating poverty the world over. Another positive impact proposed from the movement of peoples from less developed regions of the world to the more economically developed North, where the population is rapidly aging and overall birth rates are down, would be a younger populace. This in turn could shore up the entry-level work base and support social security or other pension plans of aging populations.

Despite these theories, extensive discrimination persists against immigrants worldwide. The treatment of migrants in these host countries is a constant topic of debate, and violations of human rights are rife. Interestingly, the United Nations Convention on the Protection of the Rights of All Migrant Workers and Members of Their Families, a multinational treaty, has been ratified by 48 countries. However, most of these countries are immigrant source countries and exporters of cheap, low-skilled labor. Most of the Western countries that are the receiver countries of such immigrants—among them the United States, Australia, and many European nations—have not ratified the treaty.

The perspectives contained in *Opposing Viewpoints: Peoples on the Move: The Immigration Crisis* present thoughtful examination of the many facets of a critical contemporary issue. In chapters titled "What Defines an Immigration Crisis?" "Is the Immigration Crisis Actually Several Different Crises?" "What Humanitarian Problems Does the Immigration Crisis Create?" and "What Is the Future of Immigration Policy?," viewpoint authors bring to light the complexities of migration in today's world, as well as the difficulties in finding solutions.

OPPOSING VIEWPOINTS® SERIES

CHAPTER 1

What Defines an Immigration Crisis?

Chapter Preface

T he migrant's journey can be an especially dangerous and difficult one. Every day, from every corner of the world, people make the decision to leave their homes and often their families in order to pursue a better and happier future. The large numbers of people fleeing negative situations is generally not the real problem. It is the failure of governmental systems to respond or cooperate in an adequate or orderly way that is usually the root of the problem.

The push-pull view of immigrant movements would define the migrant crisis as a humanitarian one. Those emphasizing "push" factors recognize that reasons for migration might be mixed, even with refugees being used politically as weapons. Those emphasizing "pull" factors find fault with border enforcement policies or other flaws in the management and policies in handling migrants.

The immigrant crisis is not just a current event. In fact, specific recent historical migrant crises may be considered as continual history, occuring all over the world. Some recent crises include the European migrant crisis, with the increased movement of refugees and migrants into Europe after the event of the Arab Spring political protests and uprisings in the Middle East. The United States has made headlines with former president Donald Trump's signing of Executive Order 13767, which directed the US government to officially start constructing a wall on the Mexican–American border, even though one was already standing. The Trump administration also made headlines for the separation of immigrant parents from minor children, a policy that was seen by many as a highly unethical attempt at illegal immigration deterrence.

> "Although there were policies in
> place to regulate and monitor the
> movement of people into the U.S.,
> the policies differed widely from the
> immigration policies we know today."

The United States Must Embrace, Not Condemn, Immigration

Emma Tallon

In the following viewpoint, Emma Tallon points out the hypocritical context of the immigration debate in the United States. Viewed from a historical perspective, the truth is that the US was founded by the mass movements of immigrants. For a country that celebrates its "melting pot" history, recent waves of immigrants have been subject to persecution, reaching a peak during the Trump administration. Emma Tallon is a human rights activist with Amnesty International and a former intern at NATO Association of Canada.

As you read, consider the following questions:

1. What did the Naturalization Act of 1790 establish?
2. Why did immigration policy in the United States start to shift?
3. According to this viewpoint, how has the US broken international law?

"America's Immigration Crisis in Historical Perspective," by Emma Tallon, NATO Association of Canada, August 7, 2019. Reprinted by permission.

With immigration at the center of current American political debates, it is worth revisiting the deeper history underlying the current crisis. The mass movement of people into the U.S. was a fundamental component in the founding of the modern nation, with waves of immigrants from Europe and elsewhere rapidly displacing—and in many cases decimating—indigenous populations. Although individual reasons for migrating varied enormously, most were guided by the desire to seek out new opportunities. Most migrants hoped to seek out economic opportunities, flee religious persecution back home, or otherwise improve their lives and the lives of their families. At a time when America was experiencing mass economic and industrial growth, immigration was the logical conclusion and it is no exaggeration to say that the U.S. as a modern nation-state was founded by immigrants.

Although there were policies in place to regulate and monitor the movement of people into the U.S., the policies differed widely from the immigration policies we know today. The Naturalization Act of 1790 established the first-ever guidelines for obtaining citizenship in America. However, the definition of citizenship was rather limited. It allowed for people to apply for citizenship if they were a free white person and had resided in the U.S. for at least two years. Following the Naturalization Act was the Fourteenth Amendment, passed in 1868. The amendment was adopted to guarantee "equal protection of the laws" for black Americans. However, the terms outlined in the amendment were limited and black people in the U.S. continued, and still do to this day, to face systematic discrimination based solely on the color of their skin. "Equal protection" under the laws is something that has not yet been truly achieved in U.S. society.

In 1948, immigration policies in the U.S. began to shift as a result of a changing international context. Following the utter destruction of World War Two, the number of European refugees fleeing their homes began to rise. The Displaced Persons Act of 1948 was enacted by Congress to address the seven million people that were fleeing persecution in Europe. The migrants were permitted to bring their families with them to the U.S. as long as they were considered "good citizens" and would pledge to stay out of jail. Bringing together the multiple laws that governed immigration into the U.S. at the time, the Immigration and Nationality Act of 1952 marked a drastic shift of immigration policies. The act was meant to exclude certain migrants by focusing primarily on immigrants determined to be unlawful and immoral. In reality, the act limited immigration from the Eastern Hemisphere while leaving the Western Hemisphere unrestricted, as well as establishing a precedent for skilled workers and increasing entry screening procedures. On the contrary, 1965 marked a step towards a more open immigration policy. The Immigration and Nationality Act of 1965 stated that any immigrant who arrives in the U.S. is eligible to apply for asylum.

As the years went on, the immigration process in the U.S. has become more comprehensive, and stricter regulations have been established to address the ongoing movement of peoples. Although global refugee flows have escalated in recent years—due to issues including but not limited to climate change, government corruption, and civil wars—the majority of national borders have become firmer. In 1986, for example, the Immigration Reform and Control Act (IRCA) was established. The IRCA legalized undocumented migrants residing in the U.S. in an unlawful manner and enacted sanctions that banned employers from hiring migrants known to be illegally working in America. The goal was to isolate migrants so that they had no other choice but to return to their home country. The assumption was that if they were unable to make a living in the U.S., they would not be able to continue living there.

Since 1986, countless new VISA laws have been put in place, condemning migrants for staying in the country past their VISA expiry date. The most prominent show of an anti-immigrant attitude came in 2006, when the U.S. government authorized the construction of a border fence along 700 miles of the US-Mexico border, known as the Fence Act of 2006. It was signed by President

George W. Bush and received relatively bipartisan support from Congress. The Bush administration upheld the bill as an "important step forward in our nation's efforts to control our borders and reform our immigration system."

Yet, in reality, the border acted as a physical barrier separating migrants from their loved ones.

Even under Barack Obama's progressive administration, strong immigration measures remained in place. The former Democratic administration deported approximately three million people. Ten years after the American anti-immigrant came to a perceived climax with the Fence Act came the election of President Donald Trump in 2016, anti-immigration being a key motto of his presidency. Racist

WHY PEOPLE MIGRATE

People have moved from their home countries for centuries, for all sorts of reasons. Some are drawn to new places by "pull" factors, others find it difficult to remain where they are and migrate because of "push" factors. These have contributed to the recent inward movement of people to here but are also the reason why people from here have emigrated to other countries.

Over 80 million people in the world have Irish blood; 36.5 million US residents claimed Irish ancestry in 2007. Historically some were transported or sold into slavery or left because of poverty, hunger, persecution, discrimination, civil war, unemployment and, more recently, simply for education and better jobs. Worldwide numbers of migrants have risen rapidly in the last decade. The International Organization for Migration estimates that there were around 244 million international migrants in 2015.

Pull Factors

Migrants are drawn to countries such as the UK and Ireland for the following factors:

- Developed countries, or industrialised city areas within countries, draw labour from countries or regions where incomes are lower.
- International transport has never been easier and is cheaper than ever, relative to incomes.

and anti-immigrant sentiments proved to be crucial detriments of the "Trump Vote." The broad reason the Trump administration is continuing to follow anti-immigrant policies is economic nationalism. There is a common misconception in the U.S. that immigrants are "stealing" jobs from Americans. Trump's "America First" campaign is designed to leverage this misconception by claiming to protect American workers and industries. The Trump administration's immigration policies include but are not limited to completing a U.S.-Mexico border wall, deporting immigrants who arrived in America as children, restricting travel and work visas, increasing screening for refugees, and limiting the number of legal immigrants. Trump is following that populist notion that

- The telephone and internet make it easier to access information.
- Falling birth rates in developed countries contribute to labour shortages and skills gaps.
- Extra people are required when there is rapid economic expansion.
- People are drawn to stable democracies where human rights and religious freedoms are more likely to be respected.
- Many people in other parts of the world speak English or want to learn English.
- Young people move in order to get better jobs or improve their qualifications, including their language skills.

Push Factors

Negative factors at home add to the reasons why people feel compelled to move.

- Lack of prospects for career advancement
- Poverty and low incomes
- High unemployment rates
- Persecution and poor human rights
- Internal conflict and war
- Climate change, natural disasters and famine

"Why Do People Migrate?" Embrace.

immigrants are a threat to a country's national identity. Rather than seeing immigrants as an asset to the U.S. and a triumph in diversity and unification, Trump perceives immigrants as "others."

On October 31, 2018, the Trump administration directed 5,000 active duty and National Guard troops to the Mexican border, with the goal of stopping a migrant caravan of asylum seekers from crossing the border. The migrant caravan was created in order to protect migrants from human traffickers and gangs during their arduous journey from Central American countries of origin. Following the deployment of troops, Trump tweeted, "This is an invasion of our Country and our Military is waiting for you!" Perhaps the most disheartening and jarring immigration policy the Trump administration has enacted began when Immigration and Custom Enforcement (ICE) began separating immigrant children from their parents. Concerning his separation policy, Trump declared, "When you prosecute the parents for coming in illegally, which should happen, you have to take the children away."

Under this policy, the Trump administration separated more than 2,300 children from their parents at the U.S.-Mexico border. Due to mounting political outcry and protest, in June 2018 President Trump signed an executive order to end family separation. However, he also said he would keep his "zero tolerance" regulations. The fate of the children already in state custody remains unclear.

The third week of July 2019 was once again marked by ICE raids against migrants. More than 2,000 migrants illegally residing in the U.S. were targeted in what the Trump administration referred to as Operation Border Resolve. From May 13 through July 11, ICE arrested 899 adults who had received final deportation orders. The Trump administration ordered ICE to deport 256,086 immigrants in the 2018 fiscal year alone. For Trump, it seems "making America great again" leaves little space for newcomers.

The Trump administration has recently finalized a plan that would allow them to sidestep immigration courts and deport undocumented immigrants who are not able to prove they have been residing in the U.S. for two consecutive years. Omar Jadwat, the director of the ACLU's Immigrants' Rights Project, said in a written statement, "Under this unlawful plan, immigrants who have lived here for years would be deported with less due process than people get in traffic courts."

Detained immigrants are currently being held in detention centers around the U.S., with high numbers in California and Texas. Conditions of these detention centers have been under fire in recent news, due to reports of overcrowding and lack of proper supplies and facilities. Court documents from asylum seekers in the detention centers highlight the dire conditions, citing inadequate food and water, freezing temperatures, and a lack of proper bedding. What is going on in the U.S. is not only an immigration crisis but a crisis of humanity. The Trump administration is ignoring the simple fact that migrants entering the U.S. are doing so for their safety and for the safety of their families. They are leaving their homes in search of a safer, better life. Migrants flee for countless reasons: war, hunger, extreme poverty, climate change, natural disasters, or the desire for better social and educational opportunities.

Under international law, refugees and asylum seekers must be protected. Article 14 of the Universal Declaration of Human Rights states that everyone has the right to seek asylum from persecution in other countries. The 1951 UN Refugee Convention protects refugees from being returned to countries where they risk persecution. The 1990 Migrant Workers Convention protects migrants and their families. The danger is that the U.S., one of the most powerful and influential nations in the world, is not following international law. Migrants deserve and are rightfully owed protection from deportation and detention. Immigration has been a facet of U.S. society since the origins of the modern state— this tradition must be embraced rather than violently condemned.

> *"The U.S. has had the most net immigration in the world for decades, and the projections are based on the assumption that this will continue."*

Declining Immigration Is America's Real Crisis

Adrian Raftery

In the following viewpoint, Adrian Raftery argues that the more troubling demographic changes affecting the future of the United States stem not from low birth rates but from declines in immigration. Adrian Raftery is Boeing International Professor of Statistics and Sociology, University of Washington.

As you read, consider the following questions:

1. How do high immigration rates help a country's demographics?
2. What is the projected population decline for Japan by the end of the century?
3. According to the author, from where do most immigrants to the US originate?

The U.S. Centers for Disease Control and Prevention announced in May 2021 that the nation's total fertility rate had reached 1.64 children per woman in 2020, dropping 4% from 2019, a record low for the nation.

The news led to many stories about a "baby bust" harming the country. The fear is that if the trend continues, the nation's population may age and that will lead to difficulties in funding entitlements like Social Security and Medicaid for seniors in the future.

But as a statistician and sociologist who collaborates with the United Nations Population Division to develop new statistical population forecasting methods, I'm not yet calling this a crisis. In fact, America's 2020 birth rate is in line with trends going back over 40 years. Similar trends have been observed in most of the U.S.'s peer countries.

The other reason this is not a crisis, at least not yet, is that America's historically high immigration rates have put the country in a demographic sweet spot relative to other developed countries like Germany and Japan.

But that could change. A recent dramatic decline in immigration is now putting the country's demographic advantage at risk.

Falling immigration may be America's real demographic crisis, not the dip in birth rates.

A Predictable Change

Most countries have experienced part or all of a fertility transition.

Fertility transitions occur when fertility falls from a high level— typical of agricultural societies—to a low level, more common in industrialized countries. This transition is due to falling mortality, more education for women, the increasing cost of raising children and other reasons.

In 1800, American women on average gave birth to seven children. The fertility rate decreased steadily, falling to just 1.74 children per woman in 1976, marking the end of America's fertility transition. This is the point after which fertility no longer declined systematically, but instead began to fluctuate.

Birth rates have slightly fluctuated up and down in the 45 years since, rising to 2.11 in 2007. This was unusually high for a country that has made its fertility transition, and put the U.S. birth rate briefly at the top of developed countries.

A decline soon followed. The U.S. birth rate dropped incrementally from 2007 to 2020, at an average rate of about 2% per year. 2020's decline was in line with this, and indeed was slower than some previous declines, such as the ones in 2009 and 2010. It put the U.S. on par with its peer nations, below the U.K. and France, but above Canada and Germany.

Using the methods I've helped develop, in 2019 the U.N. forecast a continuing drop in the global birth rate for the period from 2020 to 2025. This methodology also forecast that the overall world population will continue to rise over the 21st century.

The ideal situation for a country is steady, manageable population growth, which tends to go in tandem with a dynamic labor market and adequate provision for seniors, through entitlement programs or care by younger family members. In contrast, countries with declining populations face labor shortages and squeezes on provisions for seniors. At the other extreme, countries with very fast population growth can face massive youth unemployment and other problems.

Many countries that are peers with the U.S. now face brutally sharp declines in the number of working-age people for every senior within the next 20 years. For example, by 2040, Germany and Japan will have fewer than two working-age adults for every retired adult. In China, the ratio will go down from 5.4 workers per aged adult now to 1.7 in the next 50 years.

By comparison, the worker-to-senior ratio in the U.S. will also decrease, but more slowly, from 3.5 in 2020 to 2.1 by 2070. By 2055, the U.S. will have more workers per retiree than even Brazil and China.

Germany, Japan and other nations face population declines, with Japan's population projected to go down by a massive 40% by the end of the century. In Nigeria, on the other hand, the population is projected to more than triple, to over 700 million, because of the currently high fertility rate and young population.

In contrast, the U.S. population is projected to increase by 31% over the next 50 years, which is both manageable and good for the economy. This is slower than the growth of recent decades, but much better than the declines faced by peer industrialized nations.

The reason for this is immigration. The U.S. has had the most net immigration in the world for decades, and the projections are based on the assumption that this will continue.

Migrants tend to be young, and to work. They contribute to the economy and bring dynamism to the society, along with supporting existing retirees, reducing the burden on current workers.

However, this source of demographic strength is at risk. Net migration into the U.S. declined by 40% from 2015 to 2019, likely at least in part because of unwelcoming government policies.

If this is not reversed, the country faces a demographic future more like that of Germany or even Japan, with a rapidly aging population and the economic and social problems that come with it. The jury is out on whether family-friendly social policies will have enough positive impact on fertility to compensate.

If U.S. net migration continues on its historical trend as forecast by the U.N., the U.S. population will continue to increase at a healthy pace for the rest of the century. In contrast, if U.S. net migration continues only at the much lower 2019 rate, population growth will grind almost to a halt by 2050, with about 60 million fewer people by 2100. The fall in migration would also accelerate the aging of the U.S. population, with 7% fewer workers per senior by 2060, leading to possible labor shortages and challenges in funding Social Security and Medicare.

While the biggest stream of immigrants is from Latin America, that is likely to decrease in the future given the declining fertility rates and aging populations there. In the longer term, more immigrants are likely to come from sub-Saharan Africa, and it will be important for America's demographic future to attract, welcome and retain them.

> *"Immigrants have always been part of the American story, though immigration has waxed and waned over time."*

The US Has Been Shaped by Successive Waves of Immigration

Ryan Nunn, Jimmy O'Donnell, and Jay Shambaugh

In the following viewpoint, Ryan Nunn, Jimmy O'Donnell, and Jay Shambaugh document the changing nature of immigration in the United States over the past few hundred years as America grew as a nation. The authors provide a detailed report of the characteristics of various immigrant groups and demographic, economic, and educational traits. Ryan Nunn is an assistant vice president for applied research in community development at the Federal Reserve Bank of Minneapolis and a former fellow at the Brookings Institution. Jimmy O'Donnell is former senior research assistant with the Hamilton Project at Brookings. Jay Shambaugh is a nonresident senior fellow in economic studies at Brookings.

As you read, consider the following questions:

1. What does it mean that the US is a nation of immigrants?
2. How has US immigration policy changed over the years?
3. Who are the most educated groups of immigrants? Who are the least educated?

"A Dozen Facts About Immigration," by Ryan Nunn, Jimmy O'Donnell, and Jay Shambaugh, The Brookings Institution, October 9, 2018. Reprinted by permission.

The United States has been shaped by successive waves of immigration from the arrival of the first colonists through the present day. Immigration has wide-ranging impacts on society and culture, and its economic effects are no less substantial. By changing population levels and population growth, immigration augments both supply and demand in the economy. Immigrants are more likely to work (and to be working-age); they also tend to hold different occupations and educational degrees than natives. By the second generation (the native-born children of immigrants), though, the economic outcomes of immigrant communities exhibit striking convergence toward those of native communities.[1]

This document provides a set of economic facts about the role of immigration in the U.S. economy. It updates a document from The Hamilton Project on the same subject (Greenstone and Looney 2010), while introducing additional data and research. We describe the patterns of recent immigration (levels, legal status, country of origin, and U.S. state of residence), the characteristics of immigrants (education, occupations, and employment), and the effects of immigration on the economy (economic output, wages, innovation, fiscal resources, and crime).

In 2017 immigrants made up nearly 14 percent of the U.S. population, a sharp increase from historically low rates of the 1960s and 1970s, but a level commonly reached in the 19th century. Given native-born Americans' relatively low birth rates, immigrants and their children now provide essentially all the net prime-age population growth in the United States.

These basic facts suggest that immigrants are taking on a larger role in the U.S. economy. This role is not precisely the same as that of native-born Americans: immigrants tend to work in different jobs with different skill levels. However, despite the size of the foreign-born population, immigrants tend to have relatively small impacts on the wages of native-born workers. At the same time, immigrants generally have positive impacts on both government finances and the innovation that leads to productivity growth.

Immigration policy is often hotly debated for a variety of reasons that have little to do with a careful assessment of the evidence. We at The Hamilton Project put forward this set of facts to help provide an evidence base for policy discussions that is derived from data and research.

How Immigration Has Changed over Time

Immigrants have always been part of the American story, though immigration has waxed and waned over time. Immigration during the second half of the 19th century lifted the foreign-born share of the population to 14 percent. Starting in the 1910s, however, immigration to the United States fell precipitously, and the foreign-born share of the population reached a historic low of 4.7 percent in 1970.

This drop occurred in large part because of policy changes that limited immigration into the United States. Beginning with late-19th-century and early-20th-century policies that were directed against immigrants from particular countries—for example, the Chinese Exclusion Act of 1882—the federal government then implemented comprehensive national origin quotas and other restrictions, reducing total immigration inflows from more than 1 million immigrants annually in the late 1910s to only 165,000 by 1924 (Abramitzky and Boustan 2017; Martin 2010). Economic turmoil during the Great Depression and two world wars also contributed to declining immigration and a lower foreign-born fraction through the middle of the 20th century (Blau and Mackie 2017).

In the second half of the 20th century, a series of immigration reforms—including the 1965 Immigration and Nationality Act—repealed national origin quotas and implemented family reunification and skilled immigration policies. In 1986 amnesty was provided to many people who were living in the United States without documentation (Clark, Hatton, and Williamson 2007). Unauthorized immigration was estimated at about 500,000 in the early 2000s, but has since dropped sharply to a roughly zero net inflow (Blau and Mackie 2017).

The foreign-born fraction of the population rose steadily from 1970 to its 2017 level of 13.7 percent. From 2001–14, legal immigration rose to roughly 1 million per year, marking a return to the level of the early 20th century, but now representing a much smaller share of the total U.S. population. Today, there is a wide variation of the foreign-born population across states, ranging from under 5 percent in parts of the Southeast and Midwest to over 20 percent in California, Florida, New Jersey, and New York (Bureau of Labor Statistics [BLS] 2017; authors' calculations).

Though the foreign-born fraction has risen to its late-19th-century levels, the net migration rate is just half the level that prevailed around 1900 (Blau and Mackie 2017). With declining native-born population growth in recent years, even a diminished level of net migration has been enough to raise the foreign-born fraction.

Recent growth in the number of prime-age children of immigrants has continued at more than 3 percent, supporting overall U.S. population growth. By contrast, the population growth rate of prime-age children of native parents has fallen from an average of 0.2 percent over the 1995–2005 period to an average of –0.5 percent over the 2006–17 period. The population growth of first-generation immigrants remains relatively high—1.8 percent on average from 2006 to 2017—but has fallen as net migration has slowed. Thus, the continued rise of the foreign-born share of the population since 1990 does not reflect a surge in immigration but rather a slowing migration rate combined with slowing growth in the population of children of natives.

From 1960 to 2016 the U.S. total fertility rate fell from 3.65 to 1.80 (World Bank n.d.). Demographers and economists believe that this decline was driven by a collection of factors, including enhanced access to contraceptive technology, changing norms, and the rising opportunity cost of raising children (Bailey 2010). As women's labor market opportunities improve, child-rearing becomes relatively more expensive. Feyrer, Sacerdote, and Stern (2008) note that in countries where women have outside options but men share little of the child-care responsibilities, fertility has fallen even more.

Population growth is important for both fiscal stability and robust economic growth. Social Security and Medicare become more difficult to fund as the working-age population declines relative to the elderly population. Moreover, overall economic growth depends to an important extent on a growing labor force.

There are many ways in which immigrants come to the United States and participate in this country's economic and social life. As of 2014 many in the foreign-born population had achieved U.S. citizenship (43.6 percent), while others had legal permanent resident status (26.9 percent), and still others were temporary residents with authorization to live in the country (4.0 percent). The remaining 25.5 percent of foreign-born residents are estimated to be unauthorized immigrants. This is down from an estimated 28 percent in 2009 (Passel and Cohn 2011).

Unauthorized immigrants are the focus of intense policy and research attention. Some characteristics of these immigrants may be surprising: for example, more than 75 percent of all unauthorized immigrants have lived in the United States for more than 10 years. This marks a sharp increase from 2007, when an estimated 44.5 percent were at least 10-year residents. Moreover, only 18.9 percent of unauthorized immigrants are estimated to be 24 or younger, and 75.1 percent are in the prime working-age (25–54) group (Baker 2017).

There has also been special policy attention paid to those who entered the United States as children, including the Deferred Action for Childhood Arrivals (DACA) policy introduced in 2012 to allow temporary partial legal status to those who came to the United States as children, who are now 15–31 years old, who have committed no crimes, and who have been in the United States continuously since 2007. Roughly 800,000 people have used the program and estimates suggest 1.3 million were eligible (about

10 percent of the undocumented population) (Robertson 2018). Other proposed legislation—the American Hope Act—could affect as many as 3.5 million people (a third of the undocumented population) (Batalova et al. 2017).

The terms of immigrants' residency are important for their labor market outcomes, and potentially for the impacts they have on native-born workers. Without authorized status and documentation, foreign-born residents likely have little bargaining power in the workforce and are exposed to a higher risk of mistreatment (Shierholz 2018).

The countries of origin of immigrants to the United States have changed dramatically over the past century. In the early 20th century the overwhelming majority of migrants entering the United States came from Europe. Although immigrants were predominantly from Western Europe, significant numbers arrived from Eastern Europe and Scandinavia as well. Today, the makeup of U.S. immigrants is much different: nearly 60 percent of the foreign-born emigrated either from Mexico (which accounted for only 1.6 percent of the foreign-born in 1910) or Asian countries (which accounted for only 1.4 percent in 1910).

India and China now account for the largest share (6.5 and 4.7 percent of all immigrants, respectively) among Asian immigrants, while El Salvador (3.4 percent) and Cuba (2.9 percent) are the primary origin countries in Latin America (after Mexico). As of 2017 immigrants from Germany account for the largest share of European immigrants (only 1.1 percent of all immigrants).

While the countries of origin may be different, there is some similarity in the economic situations of the origin countries in 1910 and today. GDP per capita of Ireland and Italy in 1913 were 45.4 and 33.7 percent, respectively, of U.S. per capita income in 1913, but today Western European GDP per capita is much closer to the U.S. level.[2] In 2016 Mexico's per capita income was 29.8 percent of per capita income in the United States (Bolt et al. 2018). Then as now large numbers of immigrants were drawn to relatively strong economic opportunities in the United States (Clark, Hatton, and Williamson 2007).

The Education, Occupations, and Employment of U.S. Immigrants

The educational attainment of immigrants is much more variable than that of native-born individuals: there are more immigrants with less than a high school degree, but also more immigrants with a master's degree or doctorate (relative to children of native-born parents). This reflects the diversity of background that characterizes immigrants. Of all prime-age foreign-born persons in the United States with a postsecondary degree, 58.0 percent are from Asian countries, while 51.2 percent of all prime-age foreign-born persons with a high school degree or less are from Mexico (BLS 2017; authors' calculations).

Immigrants to the United States are likely more positively selected on education and prospects for labor market success relative to nonimmigrants (Abramitzky and Boustan 2017; Chiswick 1999). This selection may have increased since 2000, with disproportionate growth in the highly educated foreign-born population (Peri 2017). A few features of the United States contribute to this tendency: first, the relatively limited social safety net available to immigrants makes the United States a less attractive destination for those with poor labor market prospects. Second, the United States is characterized by more wage inequality than many alternative destinations, with higher rewards available for high-skilled than for low-skilled workers. Third, the high cost of migration (due in large part to the physical distance separating the United States from most countries of origin) discourages many would-be immigrants who do not expect large labor market returns (Borjas 1999; Clark, Hatton, and Williamson 2007; Fix and Passel 2002).

Regardless of the characteristics of their parents, children of immigrants tend to attain educational outcomes that are like those of natives, but with higher rates of college and postgraduate attainment than observed for children of natives (Chiswick and DebBurman 2004).[3] Children of immigrants receive all degrees at roughly the rate of children of native parents, though the former have a slightly higher propensity to have either less than a high school degree or an advanced degree.

Differences in educational outcomes for foreign-born and native-born Americans are accompanied by occupational differences. Immigrant workers are 39 percent less likely to work in office and administrative support positions and 31 percent less likely to work in management, while being 113 percent more likely to work in construction.

At the same time, immigrant workers accounted for 39 percent of the 1980–2010 increase in overall science, technology, engineering, and mathematics (STEM) employment, rising to 29 percent of STEM workers in 2010. By contrast, high-skilled native-born workers tended to enter occupations that require more communications and interpersonal skills (Jaimovich and Siu 2017). Among high-skilled immigrants, degree of English proficiency predicts occupational choice (Chiswick and Taengnoi 2008).

Another barrier to entry in some occupations consists of occupational licensing requirements, which can necessitate that immigrants engage in costly duplication of training and experience (White House 2015).

The gaps tend to diminish across generations. There are almost no appreciable differences in occupations between the children of immigrants and children of natives.

The entrepreneurial behavior of foreign- and native-born individuals also appears to be similar. While immigrants are more likely to be self-employed, they are not more likely to start businesses with substantial employment: immigrant workers at each education level are roughly as likely as native-born people to own businesses that employ at least 10 workers (BLS 2017; authors' calculations).

Immigrants 16 and older work at a higher rate than native-born individuals (BLS 2017; authors' calculations), but this belies sharp differences by age and gender, and we therefore focus on prime-age men and women separately. In 2017 foreign-born prime-age (25–54) men worked at a rate 3.4 percentage points higher than native-born prime-age men, while foreign-born prime-age women worked at a rate 11.4 percentage points lower than native-born prime-age women. For undocumented immigrants, this divergence between male and female employment is even more pronounced (Borjas 2017).

Women—whether foreign- or native-born—face large economic, policy, and cultural obstacles to employment (Black, Schanzenbach, and Breitwieser 2017). These obstacles may be larger for foreign-born women than for natives. Moreover, some immigrants come from cultures where women are less likely to work outside the home (Antecol 2000).

Foreign- and native-born employment rates have evolved over the past 20 years. The relatively stable levels of foreign-born employment reflect the offsetting forces of rising labor force participation for a given cohort as it spends more time in the United States as well as the arrival of new cohorts of immigrants. For both men and women immigrants, hours worked and wages tend to improve quickly upon entry to the United States (Blau et al. 2003; Lubotsky 2007).

Employment rates for low-skilled foreign-born individuals are considerably higher than those of natives. For example, 72.8 percent of foreign-born prime-age adults with a high school degree or less are employed (men and women combined), as compared to 69.5 percent for their native-born counterparts. The gap is much larger for those without a high school education: 70.3 percent of the foreign-born are employed and only 53.1 percent of the native-born are employed (BLS 2017; authors' calculations).

The Effects of Immigrants on the U.S. Economy

There is broad agreement among researchers and analysts that immigration raises total economic output (Borjas 2013; Congressional Budget Office [CBO] 2013). By increasing the number of workers in the labor force, immigrants enhance the productive capacity of the U.S. economy. One estimate suggests that the total annual contribution of foreign-born workers is roughly $2 trillion, or about 10 percent of annual GDP (Blau and Mackie 2017 citing Borjas 2013); the contribution of unauthorized immigrants is estimated to be about 2.6 percent of GDP (Edwards and Ortega 2016; authors' calculations). Providing documented status to many current unauthorized immigrants (which should increase their productivity by allowing better job matching) and allowing more immigration would increase annual GDP growth by 0.33 percentage points over the next decade, while removing all current unauthorized immigrants would lower annual GDP growth by 0.27 percentage points during that same period (CBO 2013, 2018; Penn Wharton Budget Model 2017).

The economic effects of new workers are likely different over the short and long run. In the short run, a large increase or decrease in the number of immigrants would likely cause disruption: an increase could overwhelm available infrastructure or possibly put downward pressure on wages for native-born workers until capital accumulation or technology usage can adjust (Borjas 2013), while a decrease could harm businesses with fixed staffing needs, or lead to underutilization of housing and other similar capital (Saiz 2007; White House 2013).

Immigrants and natives are not perfectly interchangeable in terms of their economic effects: immigrants bring a somewhat different mix of skills to the labor market than do native workers, as detailed previously in this document. High-skilled immigration is particularly likely to increase innovation. In addition to these supply-side effects, immigrants also generate demand for goods and services that contribute to economic growth.

However, these positive impacts on innovation and growth do not necessarily mean that additional immigration raises per capita income in the United States (Friedberg and Hunt 1995). For example, if immigrant workers were on average less productive than native-born workers, additional immigration would reduce per capita GDP while increasing total economic output. Similarly, immigration may or may not lead to improved outcomes for native workers and for U.S. government finances; we discuss both concerns in subsequent facts. Most estimates suggest that immigration has a small positive impact on GDP over and above the income of immigrants themselves (Blau and Mackie 2017; Borjas 2013).

It is uncontroversial that immigrants increase both the labor force and economic output. However, it is less obvious whether immigrants might lower wages for some native-born workers (Friedberg and Hunt 1995). In particular, low-wage native-born workers might be expected to suffer from the increased labor supply of low-skilled competitors from abroad, given that many immigrants tend to have lower skills than the overall native population.

Other adjustments could mute this impact. Firms could rearrange their operations to accommodate more workers and produce proportionally greater output, particularly over the long run (Friedberg and Hunt 1995). Firms appear to adjust technology and capital based on immigration and the skill mix of the local population (Lewis 2011). Foreign-born and native-born workers may be imperfect substitutes, even when they possess similar educational backgrounds (Ottaviano and Peri 2012).

In addition, the impact of low-skilled immigrants may be diluted (i.e., shared across the entire national labor market) as native workers and firms respond by rearranging themselves across the rest of the country (Card 1990). Foreign-born workers appear to be especially responsive to economic shocks as they search for employment: Mexican low-skilled men are more apt to move toward places with improving labor market prospects (Cadena and

Kovak 2016). Finally, immigrants—low-skilled or high-skilled—contribute to labor demand as well as labor supply to the extent that they consume goods and services in addition to becoming entrepreneurs (White House 2013).

It is therefore an empirical question whether low-skilled immigration actually depresses wages for low-skilled natives. The consensus of the empirical literature is that this does not occur to any substantial extent. Most estimates show an impact on low-skilled native-born wages of 0 percent to –1 percent. Another recent estimate of the impact on low-skilled natives (Ottaviano and Peri 2012) estimated a slightly positive impact on wages (between 0.6 and 1.7 percent). Furthermore, the impacts on wages of native-born workers with more education are generally estimated to be positive, such that most estimates find the overall impact on native workers is positive (Blau and Mackie 2017; Kerr and Kerr 2011; Ottaviano and Peri 2012).

The kind of work that immigrants do is often different than that of native-born workers. In particular, immigrants are more likely to possess college and advanced degrees, and more likely to work in STEM fields. This in turn leads to disproportionate immigrant contributions to innovation.

One useful proxy for innovation is the acquisition of patents. Immigrants to the United States tend to generate more patentable technologies than natives: though they constitute only 18 percent of the 25 and older workforce, immigrants obtain 28 percent of high-quality patents (defined as those granted by all three major patent offices). Immigrants are also more likely to become Nobel laureates in physics, chemistry, and physiology or medicine (Shambaugh, Nunn, and Portman 2017).

Presenting estimates from Hunt and Gauthier-Loiselle (2010) shows the direct impact of high-skilled immigrants on patenting per capita based on their higher propensity to patent. Increasing the share of college-educated immigrants in the population by one percentage point increases patents per capita by 6 percent. This impact is roughly twice as large for those with advanced degrees.

The total impact of an increase in the high-skilled immigrant share of the population includes both the direct impact as well as any spillovers to the productivity of native-born workers. Hunt and Gauthier-Loiselle find that spillovers are substantial and positive. A one percentage point–increase in the college-educated or advanced degree-holding immigrant shares of the U.S. population are estimated to produce a 12.3 percent or 27.0 percent increase in patenting per capita, respectively.

In an examination of foreign-born graduate students, Chellaraj, Maskus, and Mattoo (2008) also find positive spillovers for native-born innovation. Research examining short-run fluctuations in the number of H-1B visas similarly concludes that immigrants add to aggregate innovation, although estimates of spillovers for innovative activities of native-born workers are smaller or nonexistent (Kerr and Lincoln 2010).

With its complicated system of taxes and transfers, the United States is affected in a variety of different ways by the arrival of immigrants. Workers with more education and higher salaries tend to pay more taxes relative to their use of government programs, and that is reflected in the more-positive fiscal impacts of high skilled individuals. Looking separately at revenue and outlay implications, most of the variation in immigrant fiscal impact across education levels is due to differences in the amount of taxes paid (Blau and Mackie 2017, 444–60). Moreover, recent immigrants have tended to experience better labor market outcomes than the overall immigrant population; in part this is due to the more-recent arrivals being better educated, which leads to them having an even more-positive fiscal impact (Orrenius 2017).

Across the educational categories, the foreign-born population is estimated to have a slightly more-positive fiscal impact in nearly every category. For the foreign-born population as a whole, per capita expenditure on cash welfare assistance, Supplemental Nutrition Assistance Program (SNAP; formerly known as the Food Stamp Program), Supplemental Security Income (SSI), Medicaid, Medicare, and Social Security are all lower than for native-born individuals, even when restricting the comparison to age- and income-eligible individuals (Nowrasteh and Orr 2018).

Immigrants to the United States are considerably less likely than natives to commit crimes or to be incarcerated. Recent immigrants are much less likely to be institutionalized (a proxy for incarceration that also includes those in health-care institutions like mental institutions, hospitals, and drug treatment centers) at every age.

Why do immigrants have fewer interactions with the criminal justice system? Immigrants are subject to various kinds of formal and informal screening. In other words, institutions and incentives often cause the United States to receive migrants who are advantaged relative to their origin-country counterparts (Abramitzky and Boustan 2017) and less disposed to commit crimes. At the time of Butcher and Piehl's analysis, deportation was not a major factor; rather, self-selection of low-crime-propensity immigrants into the United States appears to have been the driver (Butcher and Piehl 2007).[4]

There is an important caveat to this account: recent immigrants have had less time to be arrested and imprisoned in the United States than have natives. In other words, there may be a somewhat smaller gap in their criminal activity versus natives, but the U.S. criminal justice system has had less time to detain and incarcerate them (Butcher and Piehl 2007). 30- to 36-year-old immigrants are less likely to have been recently arrested, incarcerated, charged, or convicted of a crime when compared to natives. Research examining quasi-random variation in Mexican immigration has also found no causal impact on U.S. crime rates (Chalfin 2014).

In addition to the broader question of how immigrants as a group affect crime and incarceration rates, it is important to understand how changes in the legal status of immigrants can affect criminal justice outcomes. Evidence suggests that providing legal resident status to unauthorized immigrants causes a reduction in crime (Baker 2015). This is associated with improvements in immigrants' employment opportunities and a corresponding increase in the opportunity cost of crime. Conversely, restricting access to legal employment for unauthorized immigrants leads to an increased crime rate, particularly for offenses that help to generate income (Freedman, Owens, and Bohn 2018). In total, unauthorized immigration does not seem to have a significant effect on rates of violent crime (Green 2016; Light and Miller 2018).

Notes

1. We use the terms "immigrants" and "foreign-born" to refer to people living in the United States who were not U.S. citizens at birth. We refer to the native persons of at least one immigrant parent—whether born in the U.S. or abroad—with the term "second generation" or "children of immigrants." We refer to native persons of two native parents, persons born abroad of two native parents, and persons born in a U.S. territory of two native-born parents with the term "children of natives."

2. Data is used for 1913 instead of 1910 because Bolt et al. (2018) does not include data for Ireland in 1910. The closest year for which the dataset had GDP per capita for the United States, Italy, and Ireland was 1913.

3. Results are not sensitive to whether we consider children of exactly one immigrant parent to be children of immigrant parents or children of native-born parents.

4. The intensity and form of detention and deportation actions has changed substantially over the past few years and requires further research.

"*Government officials and advocates
alike have called for state-run foster
care programs with extra capacity to
take in unaccompanied minors.*"

The US Is Overwhelmed by High Numbers of Child Migrants

Randi Mandelbaum

*Child migrants have gotten a great deal of press coverage recently in
the United States. In the following viewpoint, Randi Mandelbaum
details the process of what happens when children arrive at the border
as migrants and are met by border control agents. Randi Mandelbaum
is Distinguished Clinical Professor of law at Rutgers University.*

As you read, consider the following questions:

1. How many children were immigrants in 2021 and 2019?
2. To what agency are all children who are unaccompanied
   officially sent?
3. Can migrant children be enrolled in foster care?

A record number of child migrants have arrived alone at the United States' southern border this year.

As of June 30, 2021, with three months remaining in the U.S. government's fiscal year, 95,079 children left their countries and crossed the U.S.-Mexico border without a parent or legal guardian, many escaping dangerous and/or exploitative situations back home. This exceeds the previous high of 76,020 unaccompanied minors seen in the full 12 months of fiscal year 2019.

Behind these numbers are individual children, many of whom have suffered from repeated trauma. Legally, the U.S. is obligated to care for these children from the moment they arrive until they turn 18, according to carefully defined procedures.

But as someone who has worked with young migrants for years, I know the government often struggles to do so, especially when the immigration system is overwhelmed by high numbers of children.

Arrival and the First 72 Hours

Government officials designate a child as "unaccompanied" if they are "alone" when they arrive at the border without lawful status. "Alone" is defined as without a parent or legal guardian, so even children who arrive with a grandparent or aunt are considered "unaccompanied" and separated from these caregivers.

When an unaccompanied child first arrives, they are typically met by Customs and Border Patrol, a law enforcement unit of the Department of Homeland Security. Border agents hand the child a piece of paper called a "Notice to Appear" in immigration court—meaning the U.S. government has initiated deportation proceedings against the child. This happens even if the child has a viable asylum claim or other potential pathway to legal status in the U.S.

By law, within 72 hours, all unaccompanied migrant children must be transferred to the federal Office of Refugee Resettlement. The exception is unaccompanied children from neighboring Mexico and Canada, most of whom are quickly sent back to their country after an asylum and anti-trafficking screening by Border Patrol.

As unaccompanied minor arrivals have soared this year, the Office of Refugee Resettlement has been unable to receive all children within 72 hours. Some have remained for up to 10 days in border patrol holding cells that were never intended for the care of children, leading to reports of children being kept in cages, sleeping on the floor and not having ample food, soap or even a toothbrush.

Detention and Deportation Proceedings

Once children are transferred to the refugee agency, they initially are placed in a shelter or detention center, often with hundreds or thousands of other children. These places are supposed to be licensed for the care of children.

However, resettlement officials may resort to placing children in convention centers, stadiums or military bases when there is a sudden surge of unaccompanied minors. This began happening in February 2021 and continues to this day, causing doctors, social workers and child advocates to raise concerns that the children's needs are not being appropriately met.

Another concern among those who work with unaccompanied children is that about 75% to 90% of these young migrants will face immigration court without an attorney, according to research that tracks such proceedings. More than 80% of those without legal representation are deported, government data shows, compared to 12% of unaccompanied minors represented by an attorney.

Short-Term Custody to Long-Term Care

Most migrant children—around 80%—will leave the custody of the Office of Refugee Resettlement within a few months to live with a relative in the U.S., according to government officials.

When unaccompanied children do not have relatives in the U.S., they generally remain in the custody of the refugee agency until they are 18, when they are either released or sent to adult immigration detention.

A lucky few may be placed in a foster home overseen and paid for by the Office of Refugee Resettlement. But the federal foster system—which is different than state or locally run foster systems—does not have enough homes for all the migrant children who need them.

Government officials and advocates alike have called for state-run foster care programs with extra capacity to take in unaccompanied minors. In some places, the number of local children needing foster homes is at an all-time low.

But many states are reluctant to accept migrant children into their foster system, even if the federal government would subsidize their care.

South Carolina Gov. Henry McMaster in April 2021 directed state-licensed foster care facilities to reject migrants, stating that "sending unaccompanied migrant children from the border to states like South Carolina only makes the problem worse."

Preparing for Migrant Children

A few child migrants who are initially placed with relatives may end up in the foster system, too.

Once a child goes to live with a relative, the Office of Refugee Resettlement provides little, if any, oversight or assistance. Nor do they offer much support in such matters as enrolling the child in school, getting medical care or hiring an immigration attorney. That burden falls on families and the states, cities or towns where the children land.

New Jersey lawmakers recently agreed to spend $3 million for the "representation and case management" of unaccompanied migrant children. Only one other state, California, and a few municipalities, such as New York City and Baltimore, have taken similar action.

Most of the time these family arrangements work out. But sometimes they do not.

Recently, a 14-year-old Honduran boy who arrived in the U.S. in 2019 was abandoned by his uncle and ended up living on his own in Morris County, New Jersey, for nearly six months before local authorities learned of his plight and stepped in to help. Such scenarios demonstrate why the recent surge in unaccompanied minors puts the U.S. in a difficult situation, administratively and financially.

Yet the children are coming, whether the federal government and states are ready.

Periodical and Internet Sources Bibliography

The following articles have been selected to supplement the diverse views presented in this chapter.

European Parliament, "Exploring Migration Causes—Why People Migrate," January 7, 2020, https://www.europarl.europa.eu/news /en/headlines/world/20200624STO81906/exploring-migration -causes-why-people-migrate.

Claire Hansen, "The Messaging Battle over the Border," *US News & World Report*, April 6, 2021, https://www.usnews.com/news /politics/articles/2021-04-06/is-there-a-crisis-at-the-border.

Omer Karasapan, "Sharing the Burden of the Global Refugee Crisis," Brookings Institute, January 27, 2020, https://www.brookings .edu/blog/future-development/2020/01/27/sharing-the-burden -of-the-global-refugee-crisis/.

Oxfam, "Global Refugee and Migration Crisis," https://www .oxfamamerica.org/explore/issues/humanitarian-response-and -leaders/global-refugee-crisis/.

Zack Stanton, "There's an Immigration Crisis, but It's Not the One You Think," Politico, March 25, 2021, https://www.politico .com/news/magazine/2021/03/25/border-crisis-immigration -explained-biden-trump-mexico-478049.

United Nations, "Europe and the Refugee Crisis: A Challenge to Our Civilization," https://www.un.org/en/academic-impact/europe -and-refugee-crisis-challenge-our-civilization.

World Politics Review, "Global Migration Is Not Abating. Neither Is the Backlash Against It," October 1, 2021, https://www .worldpoliticsreview.com/insights/28008/to-ease-the-migration -crisis-europe-and-the-world-must-address-root-causes.

World Vision, "The Most Urgent Refugee Crises Around the World," March 6, 2021, https://www.worldvision.ca/stories/refugees /refugee-crises-around-the-world.

Julia G. Young, "The situation at the U.S.-Mexico Border Can't Be Solved Without Acknowledging Its Origins," Time, March 31, 2021. https://time.com/5951532/migration-factors/

OPPOSING
VIEWPOINTS®
SERIES

CHAPTER 2

Is the Immigration Crisis Actually Several Different Crises?

Chapter Preface

A nother way of looking at the immigration crisis is to break it down into components, where it might be said some of the system is working and some of it is not. Andrew Selee, of the Migration Policy Institute, a nonpartisan think tank that supports liberal immigration policies, notes there is no way for governments to "enforce [their] way out of a recurring migration crisis... Enforcement works if it pushes people into real legal [immigration] channels." If there are no legal channels, then people will just keep finding their way around enforcement.

Speaking specifically about American response to immigration, Selee states, "When something keeps happening to you over and over, you should ask why." Every two or three years, there is a spike of migrants coming north to the US–Mexico border. Yet we deal with this each time as though it's a separate incident that can be controlled, rather than looking at the larger forces at play. Perhaps the answer lies in valid legal pathways for economic migrants and an asylum system that works for people who ultimately are fleeing from violence.

To look at the root of the crisis we must examine the problems leading to mass immigration, problems that source countries should be addressing. Economic and resource issues, political strife and warfare, and climate change have all contributed to mass movement of peoples fleeing from regions that have become uninhabitable.

*"Our relatives are all considered
'aliens' … [T]hey're not aliens …
They're indigenous to this land."*

For Native Americans, There Is
No Such Thing as a Border

Christina Leza

In the following viewpoint, Christina Leza argues that tight restrictions at the US–Mexico border affect local Native American populations, many of whom regularly travel between the two countries for work and social activities. Being subject to rigorous security checkpoints impedes and strips them of their rights. Christina Leza is a linguistic anthropologist, Yoeme-Chicana activist, and associate professor of anthropology at Colorado College.

As you read, consider the following questions:

1. Why do American Indians call the US border the invisible line?
2. What is the Jay Treaty of 1794? What is it supposed to allow?
3. How do US border interests violate Indian nations' rights?

Immigration restrictions were making life difficult for Native Americans who live along—and across—the U.S.-Mexico border even before President Donald Trump declared a national emergency to build his border wall.

The traditional homelands of 36 federally recognized tribes—including the Kumeyaay, Pai, Cocopah, O'odham, Yaqui, Apache and Kickapoo peoples—were split in two by the 1848 Treaty of Guadalupe Hidalgo and 1853 Gadsden Purchase, which carved modern-day California, Arizona, New Mexico and Texas out of northern Mexico.

Today, tens of thousands of people belonging to U.S. Native tribes live in the Mexican states of Baja California, Sonora, Coahuila and Chihuahua, my research estimates. The Mexican government does not recognize indigenous peoples in Mexico as nations as the U.S. does, so there is no enrollment system there.

Still, many Native people in Mexico routinely cross the U.S.-Mexico border to participate in cultural events, visit religious sites, attend burials, go to school or visit family. Like other "non-resident aliens," they must pass through rigorous security checkpoints, where they are subject to interrogation, inspection and rejection or delay.

Many Native Americans I've interviewed for anthropological research on indigenous activism call the U.S.-Mexico border "the imaginary line"—an invisible boundary created by colonial powers that claim sovereign indigenous territories as their own.

A border wall would further separate Native peoples from friends, relatives and tribal resources that span the U.S.-Mexico border.

Homelands Divided

Tribal members say that many Native Americans in the U.S. feel detached from their relatives in Mexico.

"The effect of a wall is already in us," Mike Wilson, a member of the Tohono O'odham Nation, who lives in Tucson, Arizona, told me. "It already divides us."

Human Rights Violations at EU Borders

Europe must end systematic violence at European borders, and establish an effective independent monitoring mechanism to protect human rights, says a coalition of NGOs.

For years now, NGOs and media have repeatedly exposed how border guards and other government officials have been violently pushing back migrants at Europe's borders. Only last month, shocking images of Croatian authorities abusing people seeking asylum and other migrants came to light and caught the attention of EU leaders. The systematic nature of this abuse underlines the urgency for European decision-makers to take a stand.

The European Commission has recently proposed in its new Pact for Migration and Asylum that each member state will have to establish screening centres to monitor human rights violations. But this proposal is not enough, and four steps are needed to make it effective in achieving its aim to stop human rights violations at the border.

- Expand the monitoring scope: ensure all human rights violations committed by national authorities are captured. The current proposal risks having blind spots due to its lack of focus on cross-border cases and geographical limitation.

- Ensure independence of monitoring: task an independent body with monitoring, provide sufficient financial resources and involve civil society organisations.

- Strengthen accountability: specify how to investigate allegations as well as ensuring transparency through public reports and access to justice.

- Give teeth to the mechanism: if European governments fail to set up the mechanism and implement it properly, they must pay a financial and a political price for their failure.

Without these four measures, this mechanism risks becoming a fig leaf covering up human rights violations.

"From Rhetoric to Action: The EU Must Stand by Human Rights Promises at European Borders," by Raphael Shilhav, Oxfam International, November 10, 2020.

The Tohono O'odham are among the U.S. federal tribes fighting the government's efforts to beef up existing security with a border wall. In late January, the Tohono O'odham, Pascua Yaqui and National Congress of Indian Americans met to create a proposal for facilitating indigenous border crossing.

The Tohono O'odham already know how life changes when traditional lands are physically partitioned.

By U.S. law, enrolled Tohono O'odham members in Mexico are eligible to receive educational and medical services in Tohono O'odham lands in the U.S.

That has become difficult since 2006, when a steel vehicle barrier was built along most of the 62-mile stretch of U.S.-Mexico border that bisects the Tohono O'odham Nation.

Previously, to get to the U.S. side of Tohono O'odham territory, many tribe members would simply drive across their land. Now, they must travel long distances to official ports of entry.

One Tohono O'odham rancher told the *New York Times* in 2017 that he must travel several miles to draw water from a well 100 yards away from his home—but in Mexico.

And *Pacific Standard* magazine reported in February 2019 that three Tohono O'odham villages in Sonora, Mexico, had been cut off from their nearest food supply, which was in the U.S.

Native Rights

Land is central to Native communities' historic, spiritual and cultural identity.

Several international agreements—including the United Nations Declaration on the Rights of Indigenous Peoples—confirm these communities' innate rights to draw on cultural and natural resources across international borders.

The United States offers few such protections.

Officially, various federal laws and treaties affirm the rights of federally recognized tribes to cross between the U.S., Mexico and Canada.

The Jay Treaty of 1794 grants indigenous peoples on the U.S.-Canada border the right to freely pass and repass the border. It also gives Canadian-born indigenous persons the right to live and work in the United States.

The American Indian Religious Freedom Act of 1978 says that the U.S. will protect and preserve Native American religious rights, including "access to sacred sites" and "possession of sacred objects." And the 1990 Native American Graves Protection and Repatriation Act protects Native American human remains, burial sites and sacred objects.

United States law also requires that federally recognized sovereign tribal nations on the U.S.-Mexico border must be consulted in federal border enforcement planning.

In practice, however, the free passage of Native people who live across both the United States' northern or southern border is curtailed by strict identification laws.

The United States requires anyone entering the country to present a passport or other U.S.-approved identification confirming their citizenship or authorization to enter. The Real ID Act of 2005 allows the Department of Homeland Security secretary to waive any U.S. law—including those protecting indigenous rights—that may impede border enforcement.

Several standard U.S. tribal identification documents—including Form I-872 American Indian Card and enhanced tribal photo identification cards—are approved travel documents that enable Native Americans to enter the U.S. at land ports of entry.

Arbitrary Identity Tests

Only the American Indian Card, which is issued exclusively to members of the Kickapoo tribes, recognizes indigenous people's right to cross the border regardless of citizenship.

According to the Texas Band of Kickapoo Act of 1983, "all members of the Band"—including those who live in Mexico—are "entitled to freely pass and repass the borders of the United States and to live and work in the United States."

The majority of indigenous Mexicans wishing to live or work in the United States, however, must apply for immigrant residence and work authorization like any other person born outside of the U.S. The relevant tribal governments in the U.S. may also work with Customs and Border Patrol to waive certain travel document requirements on a case-by-case basis for short-term visits of Native members from Mexico.

Since border patrol agents have expansive discretionary power to refuse or delay entries in the interest of national security, its officers sometimes make arbitrary requests to verify Native identity in these cases.

Such tests, my research shows, have included asking people to speak their indigenous language or—if the person is crossing to participate in a Native ceremony—to perform a traditional song or dance. Those who refuse these requests may be denied entry.

Border agents at both the Mexico and Canada borders have also reportedly mishandled or destroyed Native ceremonial or medicinal items they deem suspicious.

"Our relatives are all considered 'aliens,'" said the Yaqui elder and activist José Matus. "[T]hey're not aliens. … They're indigenous to this land."

> *"It does demand serious attention—along with productive dialogue and creative thinking. But ... the only unprecedented number is the minors in detention."*

The "Crisis" at the Border Is Politically Motivated

Tim Steller

In the following viewpoint, Tim Steller argues that the current immigration crisis in the United States is anything but novel, but politicians treat it as such for their own political gain. The author asserts that politicans' hyperbole in labeling the situation as the worst they've ever seen obscures the reality that this "crisis" is actually manageable. Tim Steller is a columnist for the Arizona Daily Star, *where he won the Journalist of the Year Award in 2021.*

As you read, consider the following questions:

1. Is this article an opinion piece or factual or both?
2. Of what state is Doug Ducey the governor?
3. What does the author mean by "the rhetoric doesn't match reality on the ground"?

"Investigative Commentary: Signs Show Border Panic Is Overblown, Politically Motivated," by Tim Steller, *Arizona Daily Star*, March 28, 2021. Reprinted by permission.

P oliticians find the border backdrop irresistible.
That's why you saw Gov. Doug Ducey standing in front of the border barrier in Douglas during a March 19 press conference, accompanied by Sen. Rick Scott from Florida.

That's why Sen. Ted Cruz was prowling along the Rio Grande at midnight Friday with a passel of other Republican senators, who claimed to have been "heckled" by "cartel members" on the other side of the river.

But the border backdrop is just the familiar set for a plot some politicians eagerly play out time and again. These days, we're seeing another stage remake of the "Border Crisis" dramas we've seen so many times before.

Yes, there are real problems occurring in some places along the U.S.-Mexico border now. Many more families and unaccompanied children are seeking refuge in the United States than were crossing last year during pandemic restrictions. If the usual pattern holds, the numbers will grow for a few more months before descending later this summer.

It's a real riddle to be solved with new thinking about immigration. Instead, today's border crisis as portrayed by politicians is another version of the same play about dangerous threats that we've seen before, with a few plot twists.

Nobody has made that clearer than Ducey, with his awkward effort to capitalize on the situation. But across the country it has become a plain-sight campaign of disinformation and exaggeration for political gain.

Here are five ways you can tell today's border panic is trumped up.

1. The Rhetoric Doesn't Match Reality on the Ground

Standing in Douglas on March 19, with a wall built in the Obama era behind him, Ducey said, "I've been governor under three presidents, and this is by far the worst situation we've seen."

It isn't.

Ducey has been governor since January 2015, and just two years ago, in spring 2019, the situation was much more challenging for Arizona. That's when families from Central America and southern Mexico were filling the Benedictine Monastery, at 800 N. Country Club Road, which Tucsonans turned into a temporary shelter.

During the first half of 2019, up to 350 people a day were arriving in Tucson, Teresa Cavendish of Catholic Community Services told me. And Tucson was just receiving a narrow subset of the migrants coming into Arizona at the time.

Now there are around 80 per day, she said, and Tucson is receiving them from areas that stretch from Douglas to Yuma.

Only a couple of small towns in Southern Arizona have had serious issues so far: Ajo in western Pima County and Gila Bend, 45 miles north of Ajo in Maricopa County. Border Patrol officials have dropped off large groups of migrants in these towns that are ill-equipped to help them.

Gila Bend Mayor Chris Riggs declared an emergency in his town, asking the governor to declare a statewide emergency so that Gila Bend could tap available funds from the Federal Emergency Management Agency. But Riggs didn't get a response to the emails he sent the governor, not to mention a visit, he said.

"It's funny that he went to a place that wasn't really seeing the issue, [instead of] Ajo and Gila Bend," Riggs said.

But Ducey's decision is understandable: A politician couldn't get much buzz from standing in front of the Gila Bend Visitors Center & Museum talking about the need for more migrant buses.

Now, it's true that South Texas is having significant problems. The Rio Grande Sector, centered on McAllen, is where the families and unaccompanied children are arriving in greatest numbers. That is a real issue for them, for the Border Patrol and other federal agencies, and for us as a country.

But it's one we ought to be able to solve, and, frankly, should have by now, since we've been having it off and on since 2014.

"It's just a logistics problem," said Aaron Reichlin-Melnick, policy counsel at the American Immigration Council. "While there has been a spike in the arrival of families and unaccompanied children, the number of families is still smaller than in 2019."

Up to now, the rise in border crossings hasn't had anywhere near the effect on Arizona that the migrant arrivals of just two years ago did.

Don't take my word for it. Take the words of the mayor of Douglas and the sheriffs of Santa Cruz and Pima counties. All of them told me not much unusual has been going on in their jurisdictions, though of course that could change.

In Douglas, Mayor Donald Huish said, local churches and groups have got together to ensure migrants find their way through.

"The community has come together," he said. "Our biggest concern right now is transportation. As we all know, Douglas isn't their end game. They want to go be with family in Chicago, Salt Lake City or wherever."

Santa Cruz County Sheriff David Hathaway said, "We haven't had any kind of surge here. We've just had the usual evidence of migrant crossing."

"What is a crisis is the border having been shut for 12 months for legal border crossers," he added. "It's killing our local economy here and in all our border towns."

2. Misleading Sources and Statistics

If you listen casually to Gov. Ducey or other officials describing a current border catastrophe, you'll find they cite seemingly authoritative sources.

He started a Feb. 17 letter to the Homeland Security Secretary Alejandro Mayorkas by saying "numerous mayors, sheriffs and nongovernmental organizations have contacted my office" about policy changes at the U.S.-Mexico border.

Before the March 19 press conference, he said, he was briefed by "professionals on the ground."

At the press conference, he cited "law enforcement officials and leaders in border communities." And he made a shocking claim that "officials shared with us that the administration is seen as the marketing arm of the cartels to traffic drugs and human trafficking."

Who are these numerous mayors and sheriffs? The professionals on the ground? The law enforcement and border-community leaders? Who shared the striking claim about the Biden administration helping traffickers?

Nobody knows. I've asked but not received an answer.

Mark Adams, of the group Frontera de Cristo in Douglas-Agua Prieta, said he asked the day before Ducey arrived for an audience but didn't get a response.

"I think perhaps what we're not helpful with is perpetuating the narrative of fear," he said. "In our meetings, people aren't talking about what we don't have; people are talking about what we do have."

Citing unnamed "officials" is one way politicians mold perceptions of the situation on the border. It allows them to attribute to experts what the politicians really want to say themselves.

But it's not just this vague sourcing that undergirds the arguments made by Ducey and many others. It's also the bogus numbers they cite.

On a nationally televised program last Sunday, Ducey told ABC's Martha Raddatz that there has been a "460% spike in illegal apprehensions" for which he blamed Biden's policies.

But the figures he was citing actually counted the increase in apprehensions from April 2020 through February 2021. During nine out of 10 of those months, Donald Trump was president. Ducey did not blame Trump.

I asked Ducey Wednesday at a separate press conference in Tucson about how he defends describing the current border situation as the worst he's seen.

"According to President Biden's own secretary of Homeland Security, Secretary Mayorkas, these are the highest numbers in the past 20 years," Ducey responded. "So I'm going to stick with the data that we're getting from the federal government."

"We also, Tim—and you know this—never see numbers like this in February, in March. These numbers are 13,000 migrant children in custody and migration continues from Central America and Mexico. So this is something that needs attention immediately."

It does demand serious attention—along with productive dialogue and creative thinking. But as I know, having covered the border in the late 1990s and early 2000s, the only unprecedented number is the minors in detention.

In February 2021, there were 100,441 apprehensions borderwide. That's a lot. But in the first seven Februarys of the 2000s, there were five with more than 100,000 apprehensions. In February 2000, there were 211,328 apprehensions.

None of this is to say we aren't experiencing a challenge that will probably get worse before it gets better, and which the Biden administration must solve. But we've dealt with something similar in both recent and distant memory.

3. Border Sloganeering Gives Away the Game

If Donald Trump taught politicians one tactic, it was the value of endlessly repeating simple slogans and concepts to make an impact on the public.

We are already seeing this employed across the country to bolster the idea we are in a "border crisis." Not just any border crisis, though—"Joe Biden's border crisis," as Ducey called it. It even has its own social media hashtag: #BidenBorderCrisis.

Ducey also has repeatedly trotted out this prepared zinger: "The Biden administration has been anti-wall and they have been AWOL, absent without leave, on this issue."

Politicians from Cruz to Ducey are trying to connect the three words Biden, border and crisis in voters' minds. It happens in politics: On Friday in the Rio Grande Valley, for example, Cruz blamed Biden for the same kind of migrant housing conditions that Democrats blamed Trump for in 2019.

"We visited the Donna detention facility where we saw the Biden Cages," tweeted Cruz, who, let's not forget, attempted to disenfranchise Arizona voters on Jan. 6.

While turnabout is fair play, this is still just politics, not to be taken at face value.

In Ducey's case, his border stand is among several sweeping political positions he's taken that give away his aspiration for higher office—possibly the presidency.

Last week, Ducey's administration initially rejected FEMA's offer to establish new vaccine centers in Tucson. At his press conference Wednesday he sounded like a man anxious to keep control and claim credit for vaccines, rather than allow the federal government a role. Thankfully, his administration relented on Friday.

Ducey's rollback Thursday of all COVID-19 restrictions also speaks of his greater ambitions. The Republican activists he needs on his side in future endeavors have been demanding an end to business limits and other pandemic regulations, no matter what the medical experts say. Now he's given it to them.

And then there was Ducey's seemingly unprovoked attack on Vice President Kamala Harris. On Wednesday morning, Biden assigned Harris to manage the border situation. Ducey's reaction?

"She's about the worst possible choice that one could make," Ducey said Wednesday. "In no point in her career has she given any indication that she considers the border a problem or a serious threat. If President Biden's intent was to show that he's taking this issue seriously, he's really done the exact opposite here."

He even promoted his comments about Harris to the public, tweeting out video of them.

Now why would Ducey lash out against Harris? Remember that, if his apparent aspirations are fulfilled, he'll be the Republican nominee for president in 2024. And he might be running against Democrat Kamala Harris. If not Ducey, some other Republican candidate could be facing her.

4. Immigration Bills Reignite Jockeying

The other big political context is shorter term: Democrats are introducing a series of immigration-related bills in Congress. The next great immigration debate has begun.

For years, Republicans have staked out a position that any comprehensive immigration bill must establish a secure border before offering a path to legalization for those in the country illegally. Ducey and others continue to make that stand.

"The Biden administration confuses immigration with border security," he said in Douglas. "These are separate issues. This is a border security issue. That's step one, then we can solve immigration."

But that is a blindered view of illegal border crossings, especially those we're seeing today. In past years, most people crossing the border between the ports were Mexican men going north for jobs. Now they are families and teens fleeing Central American violence, repression and poverty.

Many are seeking asylum, which the law allows them to do at a U.S. port of entry. But they have been prevented from doing so. The people crossing the Rio Grande in boats could easily be walking up to ports of entry if we chose to follow our asylum laws.

I asked Victor Manjarrez, a retired Border Patrol sector chief who is from Tucson, about border security as a precondition to immigration reform. His answer:

"We need comprehensive immigration reform to help border security," said Manjarrez, who directs the Center for Law and Human Behavior at the University of Texas El Paso. "We do a disservice when we say it's going to be one, then the other. Ultimately, border security is getting people to go through a port of entry to ask for permission."

That's not a widely held view, though. If Republicans can convince the public there is a threatening border crisis, it strengthens their hand in the upcoming debate.

As if on cue Friday, Republican senators said they won't consider any immigration deal until the border is pacified.

5. Humanitarian Concerns Start, End at Border

Traditionally, Democrats have staked out a bleeding-heart position concerned primarily with humane treatment of migrants, not so much with who is entering the country or why.

In contrast, Republicans have taken a security-first, hard-line position, which Democrats then tend to accommodate for fear of looking weak.

But now the GOP is playing on the humanitarian side of the debate as well.

Senators like Cruz have carved out a position that says it is inhumane to tempt Central Americans to take the dangerous, expensive trek across Mexico and the border. That allows the GOP to remain opposed to border-crossing, but for humanitarian reasons.

"This isn't just a border security problem, which makes it a national security problem. It's also a humanitarian problem," Ducey said in Douglas. "The measure of humane policy is humane results. Thirteen-thousand children in custody is not humane."

That's true—it's not humane. But if he really wants humane policy, he would support the right of people to claim asylum at ports of entry and reduce the incentives for children to come alone.

Instead, he has repeatedly supported Trump's so-called Migrant Protection Protocols, better known as "Remain in Mexico," which make it harder to claim asylum, and trap people in dangerous limbo in Mexican border cities.

This humanitarian position is just a cover for rejecting migration and asylum, Reichlin-Melnick of the American Immigration Council argued.

"In many ways, I would say the concerns expressed for those coming to the border are crocodile tears," he said. "No one leaving Central America doesn't know the dangers they face. You don't climb on top of a train, 'La Bestia,' without knowing the risks. It's because what they're leaving is worse."

6. Border Manipulation Goes On

Nobody should be surprised anymore by the political deployment of what retired Border Patrol agent Chris Montoya, a Tucsonan, labeled the Border Threat Narrative.

Trump showed that it mobilizes a segment of Americans, the same segment that Ducey needs with him if he is to have any hope on his next political adventure.

The truth is, you can find something you want to call a crisis any time you want on the border. The families and children attempting to migrate these days are, almost by definition, in crisis. Smuggling attempts occur regularly—we could call that a crisis, or not.

That doesn't make a given situation truly unprecedented or overwhelming borderwide.

But these aren't harmless political ploys. The border badmouthing and restrictive policies hurt the towns like Douglas and Nogales that live off of legitimate cross-border trade and are withering without it.

That's why I found it particularly off-putting when Ducey, at this Douglas press conference, called the situation "a man-made crisis caused by elites in Washington, D.C., who are totally divorced from the reality on the ground."

In truth, he was the elite divorced from the reality on the ground. And he's not the only one.

> "The authors also found that there 'appears to be an inherent inseparability between the immigrant as an individual and immigration as a political issue.'"

The Media Displays Bias in Its Coverage of Undocumented Immigrants

Andrea Figueroa-Caballero and Dana Mastro

In the following viewpoint, Andrea Figueroa-Caballero and Dana Mastro explore the impact of negative news cycle coverage on immigrant groups. They cite a study that finds that there is a negative narrative of immigrants running deep through US media coverage. Andrea Figueroa-Caballero is assistant professor in the Department of Communication at the University of Missouri. Dana Mastro is professor and vice-chair in the Department of Communication at the University of California, Santa Barbara.

As you read, consider the following questions:

1. What group does this viewpoint state has been singled out in the news media in reference to undocumented immigrants?
2. What were the overall findings of the study referenced?
3. Does negative coverage in the news have the ability to change perceptions of all groups, according to the viewpoint?

Despite President Donald Trump's negative rhetoric on undocumented immigrants, studies have shown that first-generation immigrants are less likely to commit criminal acts than their native-born American counterparts (e.g., Hagan, Levi, & Dnovitzer, 2008; Sampson & Bean, 2006) and that there is no defined relationship between immigration and crime (Hickman & Suttorp, 2008; Martinez, Stowell, & Lee, 2010). But how has news coverage depicting undocumented immigrants as suspects and criminals affected White viewers' judgements? A study recently published in NCA's journal *Communication Monographs* seeks to answer the question, examining how crime news coverage that implicates undocumented immigrants influences biases against immigrants.

Through a two-part study, Andrea Figueroa-Caballero, Assistant Professor of Communication at the University of Missouri, and Dana Mastro, Professor and Vice-Chair in the Department of Communication at the University of California—Santa Barbara, tested whether watching crime news coverage implicating undocumented immigrants influenced criminal sentencing. The study builds on mediated social identity-based research in three ways:

- The research advances the study of the effects of intergroup threats in media messages by examining how defensive responses to crime might be intensified by threat levels.

- In the existing research, immigration itself is the threat and reflects a major frame within immigration news stories. Unlike this new study, however, it does not speak to the implications of exposure to crime news.
- Finally, the study explores the extent to which current crime news exposure promotes the "double punishment" of undocumented immigrants, through which immigrants are judged as committing not one but two criminal offenses and are treated more harshly as a consequence.

According to the researchers, news coverage of immigration has long been centered around Latinos and Mexicans in particular, and crime coverage almost always identifies Latino criminal suspects as undocumented. The authors also found that there "appears to be an inherent inseparability between the immigrant as an individual and immigration as a political issue." Thus, when an undocumented immigrant is on trial, so is the issue of immigration.

Due to the nature of the study, only White participants were included in the two analyses. In total, there were 444 participants, with a nearly even split of male and females. In the first study, approximately 42.5 percent of participants identified as Democrat, 33 percent as Independent, and 19.3 percent as Republican. In the second study, approximately 46.2 percent of participants identified as Democrat, 28.7 percent as Independent, and 20 percent as Republican.

In both parts of the study, each participant was exposed to coverage that conveyed one of three news conditions: high threat, low threat and White/control, with the portrayal of undocumented immigration in the context of the crime news coverage manipulated to comport with the threat condition. Thus, while the same storyline was provided, the authors altered the content so that participants were exposed to just one of the following conditions:

- Low Threat: The Latino suspect's undocumented status was mentioned once.

- High Threat: The coverage overly emphasized and stressed the endangerment of others, and repeatedly noted the Latino suspect's undocumented immigrant status.
- Control: The suspect was White, and citizenship was not referenced.

In the first part of the study, participants watched a news segment about an accident where a drunk driver killed a White victim. In all of the manipulated segments, the news anchor was White, photos of the drunk driver and victim were shown, and the victim's friends and family were interviewed. However, through content manipulation, participants were exposed to the differing levels of threat noted above.

The participants then completed a questionnaire that included questions about the segment, immigration and relevant policy issues, and demographics. For example, participants were asked whether "illegal immigrants contribute to the decline of society," with responses ranging from (1) strongly disagree to (7) strongly agree. The mean response was 3.58, with higher scores indicating even more negative feelings toward immigrants. When participants were asked whether "others respect my racial/ethnic group," the average response on the same 7-point scale was 5.70, indicating participants' more favorable feelings toward their own group identity. Participants were also asked, "How long (in years) should this man spend in prison?" The mean response across all conditions was approximately 26 years.

The second part of the study was conducted to ensure that the results revealed in the first study could apply beyond drunk driving to other forms of criminal news coverage. The researchers used a multiple-message design, where participants were shown one of two news segments featuring a crime. Half of the participants saw one news segment covering a murder, and the other half saw coverage of a hit-and-run incident featuring both Latino and White suspects. As in the first part of the study, the participants were exposed to three different levels of threats with both White and Latino suspects. Participants then completed a questionnaire on the segment, demographics, and immigration. The results provided more evidence that "exposure to crime news coverage featuring undocumented immigrants promotes bias in criminality judgements." In both studies, the undocumented Mexican suspect accused of the crime received a greater punishment than their White counterpart.

The overall findings from this study echoed previous research indicating that racial/ethnic bias influences sentencing. The research revealed that undocumented Latino immigrants are unjustly implicated and overly represented as criminals in news coverage, and exposure to that news coverage triggers inequitable treatment. The researchers believe that given the current political climate, these "anti-immigrant frames are unlikely to disappear from the media landscape."

The authors also note that this negative narrative of immigrants as criminals can implicate other immigrant groups, not only Latinos. For example, news coverage of Muslims as terrorists also suggests that Muslim immigrants are likely to face similar discriminatory behavior.

The researchers add that the impact of threatening immigration coverage on viewers should continue to be explored to ensure the safety and well-being of immigrants and native-born citizens alike.

> *"It appears many asylum seekers in Mexico, including Haitians, took heed of Biden's promises during the presidential election campaign to restore the asylum system."*

The US Skirts Its Legal and Moral Duties

Karen Musalo

In the following viewpoint, Karen Musalo argues that the Biden administration has turned its back on Haitians seeking asylum in the US. The ill and discriminatory treatment of these refugees is even more scathing because of the responsibility the US has in Haiti's political problems. Karen Musalo is professor of international law and an expert on refugee law and policy at the University of California, Hastings.

As you read, consider the following questions:

1. How are asylum seekers different from migrants in status?
2. What did the Refugee Act of 1980 purport to do?
3. What is Title 42, and how is it being used, according to the viewpoint?

The U.S.'s top envoy to Haiti resigned abruptly on Sept. 22, 2021, over the Biden administration's "inhumane" treatment of Haitian migrants crossing the border via Mexico into Texas.

The resignation came amid debate over the U.S. decision to deport thousands of Haitians entering the U.S. in search of asylum or a better life. Criticism over the policy mounted as images of U.S. Border Patrol agents on horseback and carrying whip-like cords while encountering migrants gained widespread media attention and criticism from the White House. Border agents denied using whips on migrants.

The Conversation asked Karen Musalo, an expert on refugee law and policy, to unpack what went on at the U.S. border and whether the Biden administration is shirking its moral and legal obligations in deporting the Haitian migrants.

What's Behind the Recent Surge of Haitian Refugees at the Texas Border?

Haiti is beset by extraordinarily desperate conditions of political chaos and natural disasters, as well as the COVID-19 pandemic. The assassination of President Jovenel Moïse in July 2021 catapulted the country into political turmoil. The post-assassination power struggle exacerbated pre-existing political violence and dysfunction. Violent gangs, often with ties to the state, are increasingly a threat.

In addition, Haiti suffered a devastating 7.2 magnitude earthquake in August, just two days before being hit directly by tropical storm Grace, with a combined toll of over 2,200 dead, 12,000 injured and hundreds of thousands displaced, many in remote regions that have yet to receive aid. The pandemic has exacerbated these woes. Less than one-half of 1% of the population has received even a first dose of a vaccine.

This has undoubtedly swelled the number of people trying to leave the nation. But many of the migrants arriving in the U.S. in recent weeks left Haiti before the recent turmoil. Haitian migrants have been trapped in Mexico for several years under various Trump-era policies that limited, and then eliminated, the possibility for them to request asylum in the United States. At the same time, others who left Haiti in years past for countries in South America have suffered from deep antipathy and racism in their host countries, living in perilous conditions with only precarious legal status at best.

It appears many asylum seekers in Mexico, including Haitians, took heed of Biden's promises during the presidential election campaign to restore the asylum system. That may have been a factor in their decision to present themselves at the Texas border seeking the protection guaranteed under law for those fleeing persecution.

It should be remembered that the U.S. has long played a role in Haiti's troubles. When Special Envoy for Haiti Daniel Foote resigned, coverage focused on his protest against what he described as the inhumanity of returning Haitians to a "collapsed state ... unable to provide security or basic services." Overlooked was his equally damning indictment of the U.S. as a puppet master in Haiti's political breakdown, for example by supporting the unelected prime minister and his political agenda.

Doesn't the US Have a Legal Obligation to Process Asylum Seekers?

Both international and U.S. law recognize the basic human right to seek asylum. The U.S. has ratified two treaties, the 1967 Protocol Relating to the Status of Refugees and the 1984 Convention Against Torture, which prohibit the U.S. from returning people to countries where they risk persecution or torture. As a practical matter, this means that people must be able to request asylum at the U.S. border, or within U.S. territory, so that they have the opportunity to prove whether or not they fit within the category of persons legally protected from forced return.

This international legal framework has been codified in U.S. law, primarily through the Refugee Act of 1980, along with later statutes and regulations. It is universally acknowledged, including by the Supreme Court, that in passing these laws Congress intended to bring U.S. law into conformity with the United States' international treaty obligations.

It is entirely legal to approach U.S. borders and request asylum. Statements by the administration that people should not come, that they are doing something illegal when they seek protection, and that there is a right way and wrong way to seek asylum are, in my opinion, not only callous and cruel but also false statements of the law.

The White House has asserted that Haitians are not coming into the country through "legal methods," which would indeed be impossible since all legal methods have been foreclosed to them.

As part of the Trump administration's dismantling of the asylum system, the White House in March 2020 ordered the Centers for Disease Control and Prevention, over the objections of its own scientists, to use a 1944 public health law known as "Title 42" to bar asylum seekers from entering the United States. This law had never been used before to dictate the movement of people across U.S. borders, which is instead the province of immigration laws. And despite the Biden's campaign promises to restore the country's asylum system, the administration continues to rely on Title 42—despite most Americans now being vaccinated—to keep asylum seekers out.

Can You Tell Me a Little More About Title 42?

Even before COVID-19 struck, Trump administration aide Stephen Miller had inquired about using the government's public health authority to shut U.S. borders to people seeking asylum. He was told there was no legal authority to do so. The emergence of the pandemic provided a pretext for the unprecedented use of this little-known law dating back over 75 years. It formed part of the Public Health Service Act of 1944 to allow for the quarantine of anyone, including a U.S. citizen, arriving from a foreign country. It was never intended, nor until 2020 was used, to expel noncitizens from the United States. In fact, when Congress enacted the initial version of this law, references to immigration were deliberately omitted precisely to avoid the use of its provisions to discriminate against immigrants.

But the March 2020 order by the Trump administration targets one group, and one group only: noncitizens who lack documentation and arrive by land.

All other people arriving in the U.S., including American citizens, lawful permanent residents and tourists arriving by plane or ship, are exempt. As currently employed by the government, this public health law has displaced existing immigration law, which allows people to request asylum. And in doing so it has also eliminated the due process protections that are part of our immigration laws.

On Sept. 16, a federal court found the use of Title 42 to expel people seeking asylum to be a clear violation of U.S. law and granted a preliminary injunction against the practice. The court stayed its own order for 14 days to allow the government an opportunity to appeal its decision.

Is There a History of Discriminatory US Migration Policy Against Haitians?

Haitians have suffered from discriminatory treatment in immigration for decades, and it would, I believe, be naïve to attribute this adverse treatment to anything other than systemic racism, which pervades so many aspects of American society. Shortly after the U.S. enacted the 1980 Refugee Act, it began to stop Haitians on the high seas and to return them to Haiti so that they could not apply for asylum in this country. This violation of international law was upheld by the Supreme Court in 1993, and the practice continues to this day. Before the border was closed to them, Haitians who reached the U.S. and applied for asylum were denied at a higher rate than just about any other nationality—notwithstanding the dire human rights conditions in their country.

After Haiti's catastrophic earthquake in 2010, the government gave Temporary Protected Status to Haitians already in the United States, thus shielding them from removal. In 2017 the Trump administration terminated the status for Haitians, giving them until July 2019 to leave or to face deportation.

Periodical and Internet Sources Bibliography

The following articles have been selected to supplement the diverse views presented in this chapter.

Amnesty International, "Refugees, Asylum-Seekers, and Migrants," https://www.amnesty.org/en/what-we-do/refugees-asylum -seekers-and-migrants/.

Michael Clemens, "Why Today's Migration Crisis Is an Issue of Global Economic Inequality," July 29, 2016, Fordfoundation.org.

Nowy Dwor, "Europe's Latest Migrant Crisis Leaves Refugees Stuck Between Two Borders," *The Economist*, September 4, 2021.

Ali Golchen, "Most Common Reasons Why People Immigrate to U.S.," US Immigration Law Center, sandiegoimmigrationlawcenter.com.

Lutheran Immigration and Refugee Service, "Why Do People Immigrate? The Different Causes of Immigration," July 14, 2021, https://www.lirs.org/causes-of-immigration.

Alessandro Mazzola and Marco Martiniello, "How Covid-19 Breaks Down Solidarity with Migrants," The Conversation, April 7, 2020, https://theconversation.com/how-covid-19-breaks-down -solidarity-with-migrants-135355.

Dan Restepo, Joel Martinez, and Trevor Sutton, "Getting Migration in the Americas Right," Center for American Progress, June 24, 2019, https://cdn.americanprogress.org/content /uploads/2019/06/20134227/Migration-report-1.pdf.

Edgar Sandoval and James Dobbins, "In Texas Border Town, Residents Feel Impact of Migrant Crisis," *New York Times*, September 20, 2021.

United Nations Human Rights, "About Migration and Human Rights," https://www.ohchr.org/EN/Issues/Migration/Pages /about-migration-and-human-rights.aspx.

Laura Zafini, "Europe and the Refugee Crisis: A Challenge to Our Civilization," September 19, 2021, https://www.un.org/en /academic-impact/europe-and-refugee-crisis-challenge-our -civilization.

OPPOSING VIEWPOINTS® SERIES

What Humanitarian Problems Does the Immigration Crisis Create?

Chapter Preface

Human rights violations involving migrants or refugees may include the denial of civil and political rights, such as unlawful detention, lack of due process, denial of economic and social benefits, and even torture in some cases. The mistreatment of immigrants can be linked to attitudes of prejudice and xenophobia as well as institutionalized bias. Because of their unique status, immigrants and refugees can be extremely vulnerable to human rights abuses, including abuse by smugglers, unseaworthy vessels, border guards and patrol staff ordered to shoot on sight, arbitrary law and decisions made against them, discrimination, gender-based violence and sexual abuse, child/parent separation, and substandard living conditions.

Once processed and settled, immigrants also experience issues of humanitarian concern. Studies have shown that immigrants' rights are abused in seeking housing, education, and in the labor market. In the United States, studies show significant discrimination against foreigners and people of color in the real estate market in applying for housing. Indeed, cycles of bigotry and isolation often hinder immigrants and reduce their ability to assimilate into the larger community, which hinders all of society. Studies show that the successful integration of immigrants into a host country is beneficial for both the immigrant and the native born.

Immigrant rights are human rights. It has been noted that shifting the focus from "legal vs. illegal" immigrants would be advantageous in further discussions about the welfare of these individuals. Holocaust survivor Elie Wiesel has stated, famously, "You who are so-called illegal aliens must know that no human being is 'illegal.' That is a contradiction in terms. Human beings can be beautiful or more beautiful, they can be fat or skinny, they can be right or wrong, but illegal? How can a human being be illegal?"

> *"Labour migration mechanisms are built with the primary aim of filling gaps in skills and labour shortages in the host country's domestic labour market, not for providing humanitarian protection for migrants."*

Finding Safe Pathways for Asian-Pacific Asylum Seekers Is Increasingly Urgent

Jay Song

In the following viewpoint, Jay Song argues that Asian-Pacific refugees and migrants must seek alternative sources of entry into countries that would accept them, mainly through labor migration, so that they do not fall victim to human smuggling and trafficking. Dr. Jay Song is a senior lecturer at the University of Melbourne and formerly a research fellow and director of the Migration and Border Policy Project at the Lowry Institute.

As you read, consider the following questions:

1. Who is the intended audience for this viewpoint?
2. What assumptions does the author make about refugees and/or migrants?
3. What does the author mean when talking about a "labour pathway"?

"Labour Migration as Complementary Pathways for Refugees in the Asia-Pacific," by Jay Song, April 17, 2018. © Jay Song. Reprinted by permission.

A sylum seekers and displaced persons have long been targets for migrant smugglers and human traffickers, especially in the Asia-Pacific region. Finding safe and legal pathways for the movement of asylum seekers and displaced persons has, therefore, become increasingly urgent.

In recent years, the member states of the Bali Process on People Smuggling, Trafficking in Persons and Related Transnational Crime (Bali Process) have shown a greater understanding of the need to expand legal pathways as an alternative solution for refugees and irregular migrants in the region. In a statement released at the 2016 Ministerial Meeting of the Bali Process, member states said:

> Ministers reinforced the need to expand safe, legal and affordable migration pathways, including labour migration and family reunification programs, to provide an alternative to dangerous, irregular movement. Ministers encouraged members to consider how labour migration opportunities can be opened up to persons with international protection needs.

Legal pathways for safe, orderly, regular, and responsible migration is a key commitment adopted at the UN Summit for Refugees and Migrants held in New York in September 2016. The Organisation for Economic Co-operation and Development (OECD) published a policy paper that same month outlining alternative pathways for refugees including labour migration, study, family reunion as well as other humanitarian visas and private sponsorships. Canada has implemented a private sponsorship program where five or more citizens or permanent residents can sponsor a refugee living abroad. Australia trialled a community proposal pilot in 2013 and the Human Rights Commission and Refugee Council recommended alternative pathways. Complementary pathways for refugees is also one of the main themes for a Global Compact for Migration to be concluded in 2018.

For labour migration to be used as an alternative pathway for refugees, the skills of those refugees will need to be in demand in the host country. Host countries might also offer induction training courses for refugees to ensure successful integration. Governments can assist private companies to sponsor refugees by providing incentives, including in the form of reduced visa fees. Ensuring refuges meet security and character requirements will remain a major challenge and government will need to work with international partners and local community leaders to address it.

This working paper aims to contribute to the policy discussion on complementary pathways for refugees and asylum seekers among the member states of the Bali Process. It examines whether present legal labour migration schemes can be opened to humanitarian migrants who may otherwise become targets for migrant smugglers and/or human traffickers. It defines the terms and identifies data and methodology used in this paper, before presenting an analysis of current labour migration stocks and flows in the Asia-Pacific. It then reviews national migration legislation in major labour migrant host and sending countries, as well as bilateral agreements and other practical arrangements, including memorandum of understanding (MOU) arrangements. Six countries in the region are used to highlight distinctive characteristics in their labour migration policies. It concludes by identifying challenges and opportunities in existing labour migration mechanisms in the region, and provides policy recommendations for governments, business, and civil society to promote safe and legal migration in the Asia-Pacific.

Data and Methodology

In this paper, irregular migration is defined as an "emerging pattern of mass cross-border movements that occur outside of a domestic or international migration regime." It includes undocumented labour migration (such as economic migrants without work permits, and visa overstayers and misusers), trafficking in persons, migrant smuggling and, arguably, asylum seeking. Labour migration includes both skilled and labour migrants as the profiles of irregular migrants in the region are unclear. Some may have specific skills and knowledge that are required in potential host countries while others may not have sufficient skills and need vocational training before being accepted as labour migrants as a complementary pathway.

Data used for this paper include the 2016 International Labour Migration Statistics Database in the ASEAN by the International Labour Organization (ILO), the 2015 Asia-Pacific Migration Report by the UN Economic and Social Commission for Asia and the Pacific, and government statistics on labour migration flows in the Asia-Pacific. For the domestic legal mechanisms and bilateral arrangements on labour migration, the 2015 migrant stock data was collected from the UN Population Division, and primary data from publicly available government websites of the selected countries examined in the paper. The 2015 UN migrant stock data used in this paper does not include the family members of primary labour migrants. Due to the limit on precise data collection and the clandestine nature of irregular migrants that are not captured in official statistics, the numbers in this analysis are almost certain to be lower than in reality.

The paper reviews existing labour migration mechanisms of six Asia-Pacific countries as a baseline study on how the international community, especially the member states of the Bali Process, could improve alternative pathways for refugees and asylum seekers. The countries are the Philippines and Myanmar as migrant-sending countries; Indonesia, Thailand and Malaysia as sending and receiving countries; and New Zealand as a migrant-hosting country.

Labour Migration Stocks and Flows

While India, Bangladesh, and Sri Lanka are major sources of labour migrants from South Asia, and China is a major source country from East Asia, Indonesia, Myanmar, the Philippines, and Cambodia send a large number of migrant workers from Southeast Asia. These migrant workers go to relatively more advanced economies such as Hong Kong, Singapore, Taiwan, Malaysia, Australia, Japan, and South Korea.

The Philippines, Indonesia, Cambodia, Myanmar, and Vietnam are migrant-sending countries whose nationals migrate both to their immediate neighbours and to more developed countries such as Singapore, Malaysia, Thailand, Hong Kong, Taiwan, South Korea, Japan, Australia, and New Zealand to seek employment. Most migrants work in mid- to low-income sectors such as fisheries, agriculture, construction, hospitality, services, domestic work, or health care.

Labour-migration trends show gender division in migrant-sending countries. Some countries send more male migrant workers overseas than females: Cambodia (61.2 per cent are male), Myanmar (80.5 per cent), Thailand (80.5 per cent), and Vietnam (66.7 per cent). Indonesia and the Philippines sent a higher proportion of female migrant workers, many of whom are foreign domestic workers. Many Southeast Asian women migrate to Hong Kong, Taiwan, China, Japan, and South Korea as foreign brides through social networks or professional match-making companies. Marriage migrants are usually heavily involved in domestic and care work but such labour is not captured in labour migration statistics since marriage migration is not considered as labour migration and domestic work is not included in the formal definition of work.

Most labour migrants are young, of working age and healthy. UN data indicates that the median age of international migrants in Asia is 35 years. Receiving countries often have age requirements for labour migrants. In South Korea, for example, workers from Sri Lanka must be aged between 18 and 39.

Economic insecurity is the most obvious cause for labour migration in the Asia-Pacific region. All of the economies in the Asia-Pacific with a per capita GDP of less than $10,000 are sending countries, while high-income countries are predominantly receiving countries. As such, labour migration in the Asia-Pacific is closely related to the low development levels of sending countries and asymmetric income levels between sending and receiving countries within the region. High levels of unemployment and poverty in sending countries also act as push factors. For example, it is estimated that Filipino households that are able to send a family member overseas are three times more likely to rise above the poverty line than those that do not. If this income gap persists alongside economic opportunities and business demand in receiving countries, intra-regional labour migration flows will continue.

Demographic changes and ageing populations in developed countries are also significant factors in labour migration. Statistics indicate that countries with high migrant worker populations tend to also have ageing populations. For example, in Hong Kong, Japan, China, and South Korea, the number of young workers (aged 20 to 39 years) declined between 2010 and 2015. Within the same period, these countries have also attracted large inflows of migrant workers to help fill labour shortages. In contrast, major sending countries such as Bangladesh, India, Vietnam, Cambodia, Laos, Nepal, Pakistan, and the Philippines have all experienced growth in their population of 20 to 39 year olds. Declining fertility rates in countries such as Japan and South Korea is also a factor in labour migration, meaning foreign workers are needed to help meet labour shortages.

Interestingly, there is an overlap between migrant-sending countries and the origin countries of asylum seekers. For example, in Southeast Asia, both Myanmar and Indonesia are migrant-sending countries as well as the origin for many asylum seekers in the region. Conversely, major migrant-receiving countries such as Malaysia, Thailand, and Indonesia are also refugee-hosting countries. The Philippines, one of the major migrant-sending countries, is an exception to this trend as it was not a source of asylum seekers in 2017, but conditions can quickly change if there is an internal armed conflict. The key conclusion here is that asylum seekers go to countries where their fellow labour migrants have been going, using existing social networks.

More broadly in the Asia-Pacific, the scale is bigger but it also shows similar trends on the strong nexus between labour migration and asylum seeking. The top ten countries of origin for refugees seeking asylum in the Asia-Pacific at the end of 2016 were Afghanistan, Myanmar, Syria, China, Sri Lanka, Pakistan, Iraq, Iran, Indonesia, and Bangladesh. The top refugee-hosting countries in the region were Bangladesh, India, Malaysia, Thailand, Australia, and Indonesia.

Before considering labour migration as an alternative pathway for asylum seekers, it is first necessary to look at existing labour migration mechanisms in the Asia-Pacific.

Domestic and International Legal Frameworks for Labour Migration

This section provides an overview of key national legislation and visa types for labour migration as well as the respective bilateral agreements on labour migration in selected countries in the Asia-Pacific. If labour migration were to be facilitated as an alternative pathway for refugees, it has to meet both international humanitarian and local business demand. For refugees, this alternative pathway can guarantee a right to work and empower them with skills wherever they go, settle or return next. For migrant-receiving countries and businesses, they would need to see the benefits of hosting refugees as a business model or corporate social responsibility. Selected countries include the Philippines and Myanmar as migrant-sending countries; Indonesia, Thailand and Malaysia as sending and receiving countries; and New Zealand as a migrant-hosting country.

The ILO found that almost 70 per cent of international labour migration arrangements in Asia are in the form of an MOU and only 15.4 per cent of these are in the form of formal bilateral agreements. Pilot Worker Schemes (PWSs) and Inter-Agency Understandings (IAUs) are only used by Australia and New Zealand for Pacific Islanders specifically. Malaysia and South Korea have a number of MOUs with South and Southeast Asian countries. MOUs are important indicators of where migrant-hosting countries such as Australia, New Zealand, South Korea, Malaysia, and Thailand see the benefits of having bilateral labour migration arrangements. These are mostly on an ad hoc basis that can be renewed after a few years of trial.

The Philippines

The Philippines sends a large number of workers overseas in both skilled and labour markets. Most go to more developed countries through legal channels with workers' protections.

The Philippines has a long history as a migrant-sending country and therefore has relatively well-established protection mechanisms in its legal system. The country has amended its Migrant Workers and Overseas Filipinos Act a number of times since it was enacted in 1995 to include more protective measures for its overseas workers. The Philippines has MOUs with more developed economies in the region such as Japan, South Korea, New Zealand, and Taiwan. The MOUs prescribe job sectors for foreign workers, along with age and health tests for prospective applicants.

While generally considered as a major migrant-sending country and not a source of asylum seekers, the Philippines has in the past granted amnesty to irregular migrants. In 1995, the number of irregular migrants was estimated at 70 000. The government responded by introducing the 1995 Alien Social Integration Act, which granted legal resident status to qualified unlawful non-citizens. The Act regularised irregular migrants, but also served as a means for the government to raise funds. Illegal aliens who had entered the country prior to 1992 could pay a fee of 100,000 pesos (A$2700) in exchange for permanent resident status. It was estimated that 40 per cent of such aliens took advantage of this amnesty program, netting the government around A$39 million in fees. During this period, most of those who applied for amnesty were from China and Taiwan.

With a history of religious and ethnic conflicts in the country, a mass exodus of asylum seekers could be triggered in the future. If that were to happen, asylum seekers are likely to use existing migration and diaspora networks overseas, including in the United

States, United Arab Emirates, Canada, and Australia. As a country with a considerable Muslim population and being geographically close to Myanmar, the Philippines is also a potential destination country for asylum seekers from Pakistan, Syria, Iraq, and Myanmar. However, a lack of viable employment opportunities means it may not attract skilled refugees who could otherwise use regular economic migration streams as an alternative pathway.

Myanmar

Unlike the Philippines, Myanmar is both a major migrant-sending and refugee-originating country in the Asia-Pacific region. Most migrants and asylum seekers go to their immediate neighbours: Thailand, Malaysia or Bangladesh.

While the 1999 Law Relating to Overseas Employment (Law No 3/99) regulates the employment of Myanmar's citizens who are working overseas, it does not provide full protection for its workers, or require migrant agents to be registered or prohibit exploitation. Its legal framework is not mature enough to protect its overseas workers, much less asylum seekers, especially ethnic minorities who escape from ongoing persecution from the regime. Since Aung San Suu Kyi came to power, the country's democratic standards have improved. Yet, the Burmese military's treatment of ethnic minorities and religious ethnic tensions have still created a mass exodus of Rohingya Muslims from Myanmar's borders.

Myanmar concluded MOUs with Thailand in 2003 and South Korea in 2008. The MOU with Thailand defines the term of employment as two years, which may be extended by another two years. However, the total employment period cannot exceed four years. It does not limit the industries within which Myanmar migrants can work. The MOU also focuses on integrating irregular migrants from Myanmar. Unlike the Philippines, Myanmar has yet to establish protection mechanisms for workers going overseas, including from potential exploitation by employers or recruitment agencies.

Indonesia

In 2015, 68 per cent of Indonesian migrants went to other Muslim countries such as Saudi Arabia, Malaysia, and United Arab Emirates for work. In the past decade, undocumented Indonesian migrants in Malaysia were granted amnesty, and were therefore regularised as lawful migrants. It is unknown how many among them were asylum seekers. Similarly, Indonesia's neighbours, Malaysia and Thailand, host a large number of irregular migrants and often grant amnesty to undocumented migrants, incorporating them through formal mechanisms to monitor and regulate migration. The overall conditions in the region means that host countries benefit from legalising irregular migrants, including long-term asylum seekers. They can formally contribute to the host country's economy and community security. Amnesty to a small number of asylum seekers who have been in the country for an extended period, who pose no harm to society, and who are willing to contribute to the host community should be considered as a special one-off complementary pathway.

Indonesia's Law on Immigration (Law No 6/2011) regulates the entrance and departure of individuals within Indonesian territory, immigration control, and immigration detention. The Regulation of the Minister of Manpower and Transmigration No 6 of 2013 facilitates the placement of Indonesian workers overseas by requiring a representative to act on behalf of a licensed placement operator in the receiving country. The Regulation also outlines the reporting obligations of the relevant parties, and the processes for dispute settlement. Government Regulation No 4 of 2013 sets out the procedures for the employment of Indonesian migrant workers. Indonesia has MOUs with a number of countries, including Japan where it sends its registered nurses and certified care workers. MOUs normally specify the worker's age, language proficiency, and health tests.

As both a migrant sending and receiving country, Indonesia has basic protective mechanisms in place for migrant workers. By Presidential Decree, the government has also established an integrated team for the protection of Indonesian workers overseas. This team is responsible for evaluating the problems faced by overseas Indonesian workers, and making recommendations to resolve them. It is also responsible for evaluating the policy and legal framework relating to the placement and protection of emigrant workers, as well as reviewing existing MOUs between Indonesia and receiving countries. In addition, Indonesia ratified the International Convention on the Protection of the Rights of All Migrant Workers and Members of Their Families in 2012, strengthening its commitment to international standards and the protection of workers' rights.

Thailand

In 2015, half of Thailand's migrants were from neighbouring Myanmar. A large number of migrants and asylum seekers are not documented. Along the Thai-Burma borders, many ethnic minorities such as Karen, Kachin, Mon, and Shan have lived in camps for prolonged periods, seeking refuge. Another 46 per cent of Thailand's migrants are from neighbouring countries, Laos and Cambodia.

Thailand has tried to legalise its irregular migrants from neighbouring countries. It entered into MOUs with Cambodia and Myanmar in 2003 and with Laos in 2002. The MOUs define the terms of employment for migrants as two years with a possible extension of another two years. The focus of Thai legislation is to legalise irregular economic migrants from Cambodia and to integrate them into the local legal framework. In 2015, Thailand and Laos entered into another MOU that focused on the elimination of the trafficking of women and children. Additionally, trade unions in Thailand and Cambodia also signed an MOU in November 2013 on the protection of migrant workers' rights.

In practice, Thailand has been carrying out alternative ways to accommodate asylum seekers from Myanmar but outside its legal framework. The danger of allowing informal alternative pathways is that the practice is arbitrary and entirely in the hands of the executives, and therefore not guaranteed in the country's legal framework with access to justice and protection. For example, the Thai government has allowed irregular migrants, including asylum seekers, to stay and work during stable times. This position, however, has changed over the past few years under the military government which has applied stricter rules on immigration. Since 2014, the Thai government has deported irregular migrants from Myanmar and Cambodia.

Malaysia

In 2015, 67 per cent of Malaysia's migrants originated from Indonesia, Bangladesh, and Myanmar. They are also in the top ten source countries for refugees seeking asylum in the region. This number does not capture the large number of Rohingya asylum seekers who are waiting for their refugee status to be determined by the United Nations High Commissioner for Refugees (UNHCR) while working in unregulated economic sectors. Malaysia is not a party to the 1951 Refugee Convention and does not recognise the Rohingyas as refugees. There are almost 58 000 Rohingyas registered with UNHCR in Malaysia, but it is estimated 90,000 Rohingyas already live in the country.

Malaysia's Employment (Restriction) Act was enacted in 1968 and amended in 1988. Similar to Thailand's Alien Working Act, the Employment (Restriction) Act regulates work permits, registration of foreign workers, and restrictions for non-Malaysian citizens. Malaysia has two different tracks for skilled and labour migration. For skilled migration, a foreign applicant needs a letter from their employer. For labour migrants, however, there are a number of restrictions such as gender, age (between 18 and 45 years old), and industry. Some industries are only open to migrants from certain countries. Foreign workers from Thailand, Cambodia, Nepal, Myanmar, Laos, Vietnam, the Philippines (males only), Pakistan, Sri Lanka, Turkmenistan, Uzbekistan, and Kazakhstan can work in all sectors. However, workers from India can only work in construction, service, agriculture, and plantation industries.

Male workers from Indonesia cannot work in manufacturing, while their female counterparts can work in all sectors. Migrants from Bangladesh can only work in plantations.

All foreign domestic workers must be female, be between 21 and 45 years old, meet religious criteria, and come from approved countries, namely Thailand, Cambodia, Vietnam, Laos, the Philippines, Indonesia, Sri Lanka, and India. All prospective employers must also submit applications prior to hiring foreign domestic workers. Labour migrants cannot bring their families and must meet a character test and health requirements. This work permit can be for a period of up to ten years, with no possibility of attaining permanent residency.

While Malaysia has MOUs with a number of countries including Bangladesh, Cambodia, China, India, Indonesia, Pakistan, Sri Lanka, Thailand, and Vietnam, it does not have one with Myanmar where most resident refugees originate. In its MOU with Bangladesh and Cambodia, Malaysia allows businesses in the service, construction, farming, plantation, manufacturing, and domestic work sectors to hire foreign workers between 18 and 45 years of age.

Malaysia is undergoing a pilot scheme that gives refugees the right to work. In February 2017, the government announced a project granting 300 Rohingya refugees the right to work in the country's plantation and manufacturing sectors. A full-scale evaluation has not been conducted yet but civil society has already raised concerns that this alternative pathway for Rohingya refugees is another form of labour exploitation. For labour migration to be a complementary pathway for refugees, proper protection mechanisms should be in place. Whether Malaysia provides such mechanisms largely remains questionable.

New Zealand

New Zealand is a migrant-receiving country, hosting migrants from more than 60 countries, with the top source countries in the Asia-Pacific being China, India, Fiji, Samoa, the Philippines, South

Korea and Tonga. However, New Zealand also receives migrants from refugee source countries such as Pakistan and Myanmar.

New Zealand's Immigration Act of 2009 regulates rules on visas, deportation, appeals and other proceedings, as well as detention and relevant immigration offences. There are comprehensive visa categories for both skilled migrants and labour migrants from certain nationalities. For skilled migrants, there is a points-based visa system towards permanent residency, where factors such as age, work experience, qualifications, and an offer of skilled employment are considered. Migrants can bring their family members to New Zealand, but must meet the language, health, and character requirements. New Zealand also has a Long Term Skills Shortage List Work Visa, under which migrants are required to have specific work experience, qualifications, and occupational registration to work in a listed sector. This list includes jobs in construction, engineering, finance and business, health and social services, ICT electronics and telecommunications, recreation, hospitality and tourism, science, and trades. This visa is initially offered for 30 months, but after two years, migrants can also apply for permanent residency. New Zealand allocates 300 spots per year for highly-skilled young applicants between 20 and 35 years, who agree to live and work in the country for nine months. They can later apply for a longer-term visa or permanent residence as skilled migrants. New Zealand has also implemented a Student and Work Visa for a period of six months to four years for those seeking practical work experience or wanting to complete study or training.

New Zealand's labour migration streams are directly tied to job shortages in its labour market. For example, the Seasonal Employer Limited Visa offers 7500 temporary visas per year for a term of up to seven months, and the Fishing Crew Work Visa is offered when there is no New Zealand national able to perform the job in the fishery sector. In terms of bilateral arrangements, New Zealand has MOUs or IAUs with the Philippines, Hong Kong, Fiji, Kiribati, Papua New Guinea, Samoa, Solomon Islands, Tonga,

Tuvalu, and Vanuatu, some of which allow work in the horticulture and viticulture industries.

The country also offers special categories of permanent residence or temporary residence to certain nationalities in specific occupations. Samoans are offered 1100 places per year while the Pacific Access Category Visa allows Kiribati, Tuvaluan, Tongan, and Fijian citizens to register for a ballot in which successful applicants are granted an indefinite right to stay. Each year 75 Kiribati, 75 Tuvaluan, 250 Tongan and 250 Fijian registrations are drawn. The age requirement is 18 to 45 years old. Pitcairn Islanders are also offered permanent residency. Some see this as a form of complementary pathway for potential environmental refugees in the region. With climate change and other man-made disasters increasingly becoming the source of forced migration, this active and targeted migration program offered to Pacific Islanders could also be a good model for alternative pathways for humanitarian migrants or environmental refugees.

What is unique about New Zealand's skilled migration and labour migration schemes are the visa categories targeting certain nationalities with specific occupations. For example, for Chinese citizens, New Zealand offers 200 places for chefs, 200 for traditional medicine practitioners, 150 for Mandarin teacher's aides, 150 for Wushu Martial Arts coaches, and 100 for tour guides per year. These visas are valid for three years and only require character tests. However, they cannot bring their spouses or children. Similar schemes exist for Thai chefs, Japanese interpreters, Indonesian chefs (100), Indonesian halal slaughterers (20), Indonesian Bahasa teachers' aides (20), Filipino registered nurses (100), Filipino farm managers (20), Filipino engineering professionals (20), Vietnamese chefs (100), and engineering professionals (100). It also allows 50 South Koreans and 60 Chileans a year, supported by their home governments, to undertake vocational study or work placements in primary sector industries for up to 12 months. Additionally, 1000 Chinese and 200 South Korean citizens can work in New Zealand for up to three years, provided that they are qualified in a skilled occupation (as defined in the "China Skilled Workers' Instructions" and "Republic of Korea Special Work Occupation").

New Zealand has one of the most sophisticated and well-designed economic migration streams. It also has a well-established humanitarian migration program meaning it may not need to open additional skilled or labour migration categories to accept refugees through complementary pathways.

Challenges and Opportunities for Complementary Pathways in Asia-Pacific

Greater regional consensus will be required for the creation and expansion of complementary pathways for refugees in the Asia-Pacific. While states will need to ensure that existing labour migration does not replace humanitarian programs or undermine national security, they should also recognise the role that alternative pathways play in contributing to the local economy and community development as well as protecting refugees' right to work. At the same time, governments will need to consider the moral, political, and economic dimensions of opening labour migration as an alternative pathway for humanitarian migrants. For a hybrid labour humanitarian migration program to work for both the hosting society and refugees, governments would need to consult with local business communities and civil society.

Promoting legal pathways for safe and orderly migration raises a question about the treatment of humanitarian migrants, who need international protection, as economic assets. The visa types studied in this paper demonstrate that labour migration mechanisms are built with the primary aim of filling gaps in skills and labour shortages in the host country's domestic labour market, not for providing humanitarian protection for migrants. Existing labour migration schemes therefore do not serve as an appropriate alternative pathway for refugees. However, a hybrid humanitarian and economic migration stream could be developed with the aim of protecting vulnerable humanitarian migrants before facilitating their labour. This new stream should not replace existing quotas for humanitarian programs and should empower refugees, not cherry-pick their skills.

Host countries also have legitimate concerns over potential threats that migrants and refugees may pose to their society and national security. Arguments are often framed around perceptions of threat and questions of identity. To address these security concerns, governments need to strengthen bilateral and multilateral mechanisms for information sharing on identity, criminal records, and past involvement with violent or terrorist organisations. Sharing biometric data and travel logs of individuals who pose security threats, as identified by intelligence and security organisations, is an area where countries can work together effectively. While human rights concerns about information sharing, privacy and individual liberty are valid, national security is an essential prerequisite for safe and legal migration as well as guaranteeing alternative and sustainable pathways for refugees.

Human rights groups have been raising issues with inadequate protection for migrant workers in Southeast Asia for many years. While pre-departure and post-arrival programs can help improve the existing protective mechanisms for migrant workers, these options are not available for refugees. Source countries for refugees such as Pakistan, Afghanistan, Myanmar or Bangladesh not only endanger refugees but also have weak economies such that the country cannot provide business environments or jobs for working-age populations. Politics, security, and the economy are indivisible. Further, migrant- and refugee-hosting countries in Southeast Asia such as Thailand, Malaysia, and Indonesia are also developing countries where adequate protection mechanisms are not always in place and political environments can fluctuate depending on the leadership. Only advanced economies and democracies such as Australia and New Zealand, and to some extent, South Korea and Japan, can offer access to a broader range of human rights protections.

Some of the advanced economies have post-arrival programs for incoming migrants. Australia and New Zealand provide support in language, vocational training, and settlement grants. South Korea and Malaysia offer employment training upon arrival. In South Korea, limited interpreting services (in ten different languages) are available to workers who attend a Foreign Workforce Counselling Centre. The Korean Federation of Small and Medium Sized Enterprises provides training to workers in manufacturing sectors. Training courses are offered to migrant workers from Cambodia, Laos, and Myanmar in the Samut Prakan Province of Thailand. Free language tuition is offered through civil programs such as the Saphan Siang Youth Ambassador campaign, which promotes better understanding between Thais and issues faced by migrant workers. There are also programs in Thailand where volunteer migrant health workers act as interpreters between migrant workers and healthcare providers.

The International Organization for Migration has compiled best practices in the design and management of pre-departure and post-arrival programs. Australia has one of the best post-arrival support programs. The government provides up to 510 hours of free English language tuition to eligible migrants on temporary visas, including Business Skills (Provisional), Safe Haven Enterprise and Skilled-Regional Sponsored visas. Targeting permanent migrants, the government also provides grants to private service providers to help settle new arrivals in Australia. This allows migrants to access job opportunities and to integrate more effectively into civil society. Australia's Fair Work Ombudsman also has the power to investigate workplace complaints.

Engagement with Businesses and Civil Society

Utilising labour migration as a complementary pathway for refugees is an innovative idea that requires a whole-of-nation approach. Governments should actively work with businesses to come up with best practices to build business models that encourage greater corporate social responsibility by hiring qualified and eligible refugees. With closer and regular consultation with local businesses on their workforce needs and security concerns, governments and businesses can learn from each other and work together to protect and empower refugees in their communities. Socially responsible businesses can monitor their peers for any potential malpractices or abuses of foreign workers and refugees.

The pilot program for granting 300 Rohingyas the right to work in Malaysia is a good test case. The program was initiated by UNHCR staff. The rationale behind the program was that, first, there was local business demand in manufacturing and plantation for foreign labour and, second, Rohingya refugees were already residing in the country and working in the shadow economy as irregular migrants. Malaysia does not recognise refugees. Many other Southeast Asian states have not signed the Refugee Convention in fear of more asylum seekers entering their territory uncontrolled. To use labour migration as an alternative pathway for refugees in Southeast Asia, governments would need support from their business communities. As of May 2017, not many businesses are registered to join the pilot program and only half of the quota has been filled.

Civil society is another important stakeholder for complementary pathways. Service providers can help integrate newly arrived migrants and offer them induction or training courses with government support. Human rights groups can monitor the working conditions and general welfare of refugees. Academics can conduct in-depth research on their local integration and contribution to their own communities. Governments can work with these various stakeholders to assess and update the program. Information can be shared with other states.

Regional Development

If successful, labour migration as a complementary pathway for refuges can go beyond its personal and community development and bring broader effects on regional development. Critics rightly caution that selecting skilled refugees has a long-term risk of creating a "brain drain" in countries of origin. However, new skills and knowledge acquired from labour migration as a complementary pathway in the host country can generate new networks and information between origin and host communities and increase communication and trade between the two. It can benefit both migrants and host countries. Complementary pathways through employment can allow refugees to integrate into the host society. When and if refugees want to return to their countries of origin, they can help rebuild the community with new skills and contribute to post-conflict resolution. For host countries, giving refugees alternative pathways through jobs can divert asylum seekers' choice of dangerous and illegal routes of arrivals through smuggling to safe and legal migration, which is more predictable and manageable. Governments must outsmart and offer a better, safer, and legal business model than refugee-smugglers who seek profits by exploiting desperate asylum seekers who pay. Visa fees for alternative pathways will be a critical factor for both asylum seekers and local businesses who will sponsor them. The fees will need to be more affordable than smuggling fees.

There are potential conflicts between source and host countries in using labour migration as an alternative route to settlement for refugees. Its selectiveness may create a tension between the two governments that can strain political and diplomatic relations. Receiving refugees is fundamentally a political decision. Malaysia has publicly criticised the Myanmar government for mistreating Rohingyas.

Strengthening the Bali Process

The Bali Process can play a significant role in strengthening the regional mechanism to stop migrant smuggling and human trafficking. Australia can contribute in a number of ways to safe and legal migration in the Asia-Pacific. First, Australia, as one of the two co-chairs of the Bali Process, can initiate expanding its mandates to include forced migration, recognising forced and irregular migration are highly interrelated. The 2016 Declaration acknowledged the growing scale and complexity of irregular migration challenges, including smuggled or trafficked asylum seekers. Recognising and incorporating mixed migration in its formal mandates and procedures would mean member states can be better equipped with adequate policies to tackle irregular and forced migration in the region within the Bali Process framework.

Second, Australia can continue to offer legal training and technical assistance to major migrant-sending countries such as Myanmar and Bangladesh to strengthen their domestic legal frameworks on labour migration, bilaterally and multilaterally through the Bali Process. In particular, regulating mass movements of people for economic or humanitarian purposes will help migrants to operate within legal norms and governments to monitor their progress in a transparent manner. This would also disincentivise migrant smugglers and instead encourage entrepreneurial individuals to use legal mechanisms. Through the Bali Process, Australia can initiate working-level discussions about what best hybrid economic and humanitarian migration mechanisms can coexist, in close coordination with both migrant sending and receiving countries.

Third, Australia can help strengthen the legal migration regimes in the Asia-Pacific to protect vulnerable migrants, whether they are foreign labourers or refugees, and guarantee access to legal justice for the protection of minimum human rights and labour standards. No country is free from human rights abuses. Australia is strong in establishing criminal justice among the member states of the Bali Process. The next steps forward will be to help set up a system that ensures migrant-centric access to legal migratory procedures, justice mechanisms, and victim protection.

Fourth, legal training and technical assistance must include how to simplify the migration process, making it easier and more accessible for labour migrants and reduce administrative fees so that asylum seekers do not fall into the hands of traffickers or smugglers who purport to offer a faster, easier and cheaper service than conventional routes. Making the entire process of labour and humanitarian migration easy, accessible, and affordable is beneficial not only for migrants to safely move to another country but also for the state to stop irregular migration and make national borders more secure.

Fifth, Australia is in a good position to lead international cooperation with other countries in the Asia-Pacific in terms of data gathering and intelligence sharing about trafficking and smuggling networks. In the past few years, Australia has established its international reputation on strong border security, which is one significant pillar of safe and legal migration that the region aims to achieve as a common goal. Australia can lead on best practices for border security that is consistent with international law and humanitarian principles for protecting refugees.

Sixth, Australia can work with business leaders and private sponsors who are willing to offer temporary placements for refugees and asylum seekers. Pilot programs have been in place in Australia and in Malaysia since 2013. The effectiveness and sustainability of these complementary pathways should be evaluated. Hybrid visa types can be further discussed in consultation with business leaders, humanitarian migration experts, civil society representatives and, most importantly, refugees themselves who have gone through the pilot programs. Australia can lead this discussion and offer a highly innovative and pragmatic solution to refugee/migration crises in the region and beyond.

Seventh, Australia should continue to lead the discussion on complementary pathways. No one system or pathway will fit all refugees and asylum seekers. There should be more debates on various legal pathways for refugees, including student visas or family reunions. Where necessary, temporary labour migration should also be considered. Governments should also be willing to take criticism on its pragmatic and functionalist approach. Public debates on the subject are much needed.

At the upcoming United Nations Global Compacts on refugees and migrants, Australia can be a regional voice from the Asia-Pacific, recognising the current global challenges of mixed migration of refugees and irregular migrants and bring innovative solutions to safe, legal, and affordable pathways to vulnerable humanitarian and economic migrants. The emphasis on the role of the private sector in protecting forced and other irregular migrants is central.

Conclusion

This working paper reviewed existing labour migration regimes in the Asia-Pacific region to see whether there are any potential complementary pathways for humanitarian migrants in the future. There are significant overlaps between the countries where refugees seek asylum and where economic migrants have been looking for employment. Both humanitarian and economic migrants move to their immediate neighbouring countries to seek protection and employment. Most migrant workers from Myanmar cross the borders to Thailand. Indonesian workers go to Malaysia. Many Karen, Kachin, Mon, Shan, and Rohingya refugees live in Thailand and Malaysia. A much smaller number of refugees venture into more advanced economies such as Australia, Japan, South Korea, or New Zealand.

Legal labour migration mechanisms in the Asia-Pacific are mostly temporary in nature with certain restrictions on: (1) the number of migrants; (2) nationalities; (3) age and sex; and (4) within designated industries. Most countries that receive labour migrants also require candidates to pass health and character tests. Often, migrants are also required to have certain levels of language proficiency. South Korea even has weight and height requirements for labour migration. Of the countries considered in this paper, New Zealand has the most comprehensive framework for labour migration, targeting certain nationalities and occupations in a given period with potential permanent settlement pathways. It also has labour migration schemes specifically targeting Pacific Islanders.

Labour migration is designed to mobilise foreign labour and talents, not to offer protection for vulnerable migrants. The existing labour migration mechanisms often do not fully comply with international labour or human rights standards. In order to use labour migration as an alternative pathway for refugees, a new hybrid program needs to be invented: a business-sponsored and government-administered humanitarian and labour migration program that is safe, legal, and affordable for refugees and asylum seekers. For this, governments need to consult with local business communities that will hire refugees and civil society that will provide induction and training courses with government subsidies.

The Bali Process is an ideal regional mechanism to discuss the current labour migration mechanisms and potential hybrid humanitarian and labour migration programs. Australia is in a perfect position to lead this discussion at the upcoming Global Compacts for refugees and migrants in 2018. It has tested a community support program and helped establish strong criminal justice mechanisms to stop human trafficking and migrant smuggling. The time is ripe for Australia to move forward and lead a new initiative on complementary pathways for refugees.

> *"Because of DACA, I thought we were moving in the right direction. Now it seems that we're going backwards."*

The Undocumented Must Live a Life in the Shadows

Liz Mineo

In the following viewpoint, Liz Mineo presents the individual stories of four Deferred Action for Childhood Arrivals (DACA) policy beneficiaries, informally known as "Dreamers." The viewpoint details the experiences of very different individuals and why they would like to remain in the United States, for most the only home they have ever known. Liz Mineo is an award-winning staff writer at the Harvard Gazette.

As you read, consider the following questions:

1. What is DACA?
2. How are these college students different from American-born college students?
3. Why do you think the author collected these stories?

"Ask the Undocumented," by Liz Mineo, *Harvard Gazette*, May 4, 2017. Reprinted by permission.

When Jin Park '18 was growing up in New York City, his family always told him to be mindful of his surroundings, to keep quiet about being undocumented, and to avoid busy streets where he might encounter immigration agents.

Park can relax somewhat now because he can remain in the United States under President Obama's 2012 Deferred Action for Childhood Arrivals (DACA). President Trump, a vocal critic of illegal immigration, nonetheless has affirmed the policy that keeps such students here and in school.

Still, Park worries about family members and friends who aren't covered by such a policy and may face the threat of deportation down the road. The Trump administration has promised to toughen enforcement strictures on U.S. immigration policies and to tighten the nation's borders.

Park is one of four undocumented Harvard undergraduates who spoke with the *Gazette* about their challenges, their concerns, and their hopes under the new administration. Here are their everyday lives, in their own words.

Jin Park '18: My Story

"I was born in South Korea. I came to this country, brought by my parents, when I was 7 years old. I grew up in New York. Since early on, I loved learning. I never hated going to school. And since early on, I also knew that there were some aspects of our lives that were out of bounds. I knew that my family couldn't get a car, that we didn't have health care, and that we should avoid busy streets, where immigration raids often take place. I remember feeling all of that was strange, but I didn't quite understand it. Feelings of exclusion have always been part of my childhood. I found out my legal status when, after applying for an internship at a hospital in Manhattan, the person who interviewed me said, 'Sorry, Jin. We don't allow illegal aliens to take part in the program.'

"After that, I wanted to keep things quiet, but I continued to study hard. When Obama announced DACA in 2012, he singlehandedly changed my life. Without DACA, I'm vulnerable. DACA helped me walk without fear because I was protected from deportation. I applied to 34 schools. I knew that some schools were not going to accept me because I was undocumented. When I was accepted to Harvard, my parents felt it was a validation of our lives here. For them, it was like, 'This is why we came here; this is why we went through all the things we went through.' Every day, they tell me how proud they are of me.

"I hope the administration doesn't pull families apart, and people will be more willing to understand the complexity of immigration. It's not only a security issue or a Mexican issue. No one talks about Asian undocumented students. I don't expect people to know. If I weren't undocumented, I wouldn't know how broken the immigration system is. I hope that people understand that a wall is not the solution.

"My other hope is to become a doctor to work on policies to help the most vulnerable. When I was 11, I had to search online how to treat a burn at home because my father had been burned at work and couldn't go to the hospital. I want to help people have access to health care. And finally, my hope is to live and die here. I'm an American. This is my home."

Laura Veira-Ramirez '20: My Story

"I was born in Colombia. I came here when I was 3 years old. I grew up in Connecticut. I knew I was undocumented while growing up. My parents didn't drive because they didn't have a license and couldn't afford a car. My first memory of being undocumented was when I was in first grade. It was a rainy day, and I had to attend a school concert. We walked to school, and I was late and drenched. I was supposed to be in the front row, but because I was late I was put in the back. It was a horrible experience.

"I was not supposed to talk about our status. I couldn't even tell my best friend about it. Many people assumed that I was documented. When I was a freshman in high school, someone asked me if green cards (given to U.S. permanent residents) were green. I didn't know, but I said yes, they were green. I lied and felt bad. When DACA came out, I was in my last year of middle school. It opened a lot of doors and offered me protection from deportation. I felt invincible. I felt that no one could touch me because I was lawfully here.

"After my status was legal, I felt comfortable engaging in activism, and I got involved with Connecticut Students for a Dream. I went to a meeting and shared my story. It was empowering. At my high school graduation last year, I was the valedictorian and gave a speech about my being undocumented, because I wanted to show how much you could accomplish even though you may be undocumented. I had the highest GPA in my class, and because of my grades, I thought they were enough to overcome the barrier of being undocumented. But the difference between applying for college as an undocumented person and a documented person is huge.

"Because of DACA, I thought we were moving in the right direction. Now it seems that we're going backwards. Now I'm OK because I can get through college, but I can't study abroad, which is really sad. I'm hopeful that an opportunity will come along, that I can figure out a way. I may get a work visa after graduation. But I'm not sure about my life.

"Immigration reform would be great, but now I just hope that everything continues the same. I know it's a low bar, but given the circumstances, I don't know what to expect. I would like to see the government pass something that benefits others, not only the Dreamers, because it's dividing the community. Dreamers are portrayed as the good ones, and what about the rest? Immigrants in general commit fewer crimes than native-born Americans. And yet they continue criminalizing our community."

Bruno Villegas McCubbin '19: My Story

"I was born in Peru. I came here at age 6. I grew up in California. My uncle lived there, and when the economy got bad in Peru, he persuaded my dad to move there. Growing up, I felt I had two lives. School was a very good place where I felt really happy, and everything was stable. Then I'd come home, and there was always insecurity about work and finances. When I was little, I thought the problem was money, but when I asked my parents why they couldn't get a job that paid more, they told me we why. They told me we had to be cautious.

"It's hurtful being undocumented because you have to hide an integral part of your identity. I had the feeling of being stuck. I was excelling at school, but I didn't see any pathways for me. I did well there because I liked it, but also because I didn't want to cause more anguish to my parents, who were already struggling. In 2008, when the recession hit, my dad lost his job, and we went through hard times. That's when I truly realized my life was different from others. I had to make up excuses to my friends because I couldn't do things with them, either because I had no money or I had to take care of my little sister. My father worked at anything he could; my mom was a helper in a nursing home. When my parents kept losing their jobs due to the recession, we started moving from place to place.

"Growing up was hard. I felt I couldn't win no matter what I did. You go through your life hearing about immigration reform, year after year, and you go through disappointment after disappointment. When the Dream Act initially failed in 2010, it was a huge letdown. When DACA came out, I was a sophomore in high school. It was a huge deal, surreal. I couldn't believe it. It was at last an opening. When the news came out, my mom asked me to explain it to her. It was big, at least for us, the kids, if not for the parents. My mom was happy to see that her children's lives could improve. My dad encouraged me to apply to Harvard. He said, 'I have faith in you.' And when I was accepted to Harvard, he freaked out, and so did I. With my coming to Harvard, both my parents felt their sacrifice had paid off, but they had never come to campus.

"At this point, I hope for anything that can help alleviate the situation. I feel that it's really difficult for comprehensive immigration reform to happen right now. The topic of immigration is so toxic. I do hope that DACA remains as it is. I hope that

Dreamers like myself will continue to have the opportunity to go to school and become productive members of society, and hopefully in the future there will be a program to help our family members. I hope to finish my degree and become an immigration lawyer to help my family and my community because I'm someone who understands the issue at a very personal level."

Brenda Esqueda Morales '20: My Story

"I was born in Mexico. They brought me in a truck when I was 6 years old. My parents crossed the desert later, and we moved to Nebraska, where we put down roots. I was always aware of our legal status because my parents told us to be cautious and stay out of trouble and avoid drawing attention. I've always loved school. I've always wanted to go to college, even though people said I didn't have any chance because I didn't have papers. My dad works as a landscaper, and my mother cleans houses, and they've always encouraged me to go to college. I had amazing teachers in middle and high school who knew about my status and encouraged me to keep thinking about college.

"As I got older, I realized the odds were against me. The system wasn't designed for people like me. But that little, brown, undocumented kid inside me kept saying, 'You should apply for college.' In high school, I had an amazing counselor, Antonio Perez, who changed my life. He helped me realize what I needed to do to go to college. I had to work 100 times more than the other kids. So I did.

"My senior year in high school was hard because my dad was placed in deportation proceedings. One day, ICE (Immigration and Customs Enforcement) agents came to our house looking for a relative who was living with us. They arrested him and they also took my dad, who opened the door. Around that time, I became a DACA recipient, but it was scary. I had to go to the same ICE office that was going to take my dad away. I was worried about giving all my information to the government. I also wondered what the catch was, and why it was that I could be protected from deportation but not my parents. It didn't feel safe, but now I realize I'm in a much better position as a DACA recipient.

"Around that time, I also got involved with activism. With a group of Dreamers, we lobbied against a bill in Nebraska that prevented young undocumented immigrants with college degrees from obtaining professional and commercial licenses. We wrote to senators, worked with the community, and we got the bill changed.

"My dad was supposed to be deported in my senior year, but his hearing kept being delayed, and he was able to be at my high school graduation. It was one of the happiest days of my life. When I was accepted to Harvard, I was flabbergasted. My parents were very proud. We didn't have money to fly, but my dad wanted to see his kid off to college. He said, 'It's a memory we have to have.' We rented a car and drove from Omaha. It took us two days.

"My dad's legal situation still worries me. He had a hearing on March 1, but he's safe for now. I've always wanted to go back home after graduating from college, but if my dad were deported, I might not have anything to go back to. Since President Trump was elected, I've been dealing with so much pain, frustration, and helplessness. It was hard to focus on homework when my family could have been taken away. I kept asking, 'How am I going to get through this?' And more importantly, 'How are they going to get through this? My father's hearing keeps being delayed. I don't know if he's going to be deported.

"It's hard to be hopeful now. I'm in survival mode. Even though I've been trying to prepare myself for it, it's never something you can prepare for. It feels like something is circling on you, and at any moment it could be at your doorstep. I feel very privileged to be here. Back home, they don't have the Harvard name; they don't have the prestige or the connections. It worries me more that whatever is closing in, it's going to home in on my family first, and then me. I hope they let my dad stay here. I wish my parents would be at my siblings' high school graduations. I wish I could take mom to Disney World. In an ideal world, we'd all stay together. I'd get married and have kids, and my kids would be able to meet their grandparents."

> "*Too often, police forces see the crime, not the person, they see them as illegal immigrants.*"

The Migration Crisis Is Forcing People into Human Trafficking

Jennifer Rankin

In the following viewpoint, Jennifer Rankin describes how immigrants, especially children, are being doubly victimized by human traffickers to force them into modern-day slavery and sexual exploitation across Europe as the migration crisis grows. Jennifer Rankin is the Guardian's Brussels correspondent and has also written for Reuters, the Irish Times, *the* Moscow Times, *and the* Economist.

As you read, consider the following questions:

1. What is human trafficking?
2. Who, according to the author, is most likely to be victimized by criminal gangs and traffickers?
3. How is the migration crisis being used in Europe to profit from human trafficking?

Criminal gangs are taking advantage of Europe's migration crisis to force more people into sex work and other types of slavery, according to an EU report on human trafficking.

Children have become a preferred target for traffickers, the report warns, amid growing concern over the fate of unaccompanied child refugees who have disappeared from official view since arriving in Europe.

Almost 96,000 unaccompanied children claimed asylum in Europe in 2015, about one-fifth of the total number of child refugees. But at least 10,000 unaccompanied children have dropped off the radar of official agencies since arriving in Europe, the EU police agency reported in January. German authorities reported earlier this year that 4,700 children had been lost to officials, while up to 10 children a week are reported missing in Sweden.

Modern-Day Slavery

More than 1.2 million people are victims of slavery in Europe, a figure boosted by human traffickers exploiting migrants seeking to reach the EU, according to new figures released Tuesday.

The Global Slavery Index 2016, published by anti-slavery organization the Walk Free Foundation, says that 1,243,400 people are enslaved in Europe, victims of human trafficking, forced labor, forced marriage and sexual exploitation. According to the study, 65 percent of the total are EU citizens, most of them from Eastern Europe.

European slavery accounts for a small percentage of the global total, according to the study. It says 45.8 million people are enslaved across the globe, 28 percent higher than previously estimated.

Migrants are increasingly vulnerable to trafficking and criminal exploitation, said Fiona David, executive director of global research at the Walk Free Foundation.

"You have this very, very large group of people who are in incredible distress and coming from trauma in their home country," David said. "They're on the move, they're carrying their belongings and their children with them across very long distances. There's no clear legal way for them to move."

The report from the European commission, which will be published on Thursday, does not attempt to estimate how many may have fallen victim to criminal gangs, but warns that the phenomenon of child trafficking "has been exacerbated by the ongoing migration crisis." Children are at high risk of being doubly victimised, it says, because they are treated as perpetrators of crimes if they are found by the authorities.

"Organised crime groups choose to traffic children as they are easy to recruit and quick to replace, they can also keep under their control child victims relatively cheaply and discreetly," states an EU working document seen by the *Guardian*. Trafficked children aged between six months and 10 years are bought and sold for sums ranging from €4,000 (£3,000) to €8,000, although amounts of up to €40,000 have been reported in some cases.

With limited resources, many rely on people smugglers to escape to Europe. Some resort to "survival sex" or other extreme measures in order to pay for their journey.

"What we're seeing … is they're being approached on a daily basis by people offering work or marriage; some are offering cash in exchange for blood, or body parts or organs," David said.

In a March survey, the International Organization for Migration found that 7.2 percent of migrants traveling along the eastern Mediterranean route reported experiences with human trafficking. These included being forced to work against their will and being held against their will.

Andrew Forrest, chairman and founder of the Walk Free Foundation, called upon the world's leading governments to take action against modern slavery.

"I believe in the critical role of our leaders in government, business and civil society," Forrest said in a statement. "Through our responsible use of power, strength of conviction, determination and collective will, we all can lead the world to end slavery."

"Migration Crisis Adds to Europe's Slavery Problem: Report," by Kaley Johnson, Politico, May 30, 2016.

EU authorities registered 15,846 victims of human trafficking in 2013-14, including 2,375 children, but the report's authors believe the true number of victims is far higher. More than two-thirds (67%) of people were trafficked into sex work; about one-fifth (21%) were put into forced labour, often as agricultural workers, a form of slavery that disproportionately affected men. The remainder of trafficking victims faced an equally grim catalogue of exploitation, ranging from domestic servitude to forced begging.

The authors sounded the alarm about the "worryingly sharp increase" in Nigerian women and girls arriving in Italy from Libya. The Italian authorities have reported a 300% year-on-year increase in the number of Nigerian victims of trafficking.

Traffickers are increasingly exploiting legal migration routes by persuading non-EU nationals to apply for asylum or a residence permit.

More than two-thirds of the identified victims were EU nationals, with the largest numbers coming from Romania, Bulgaria, the Netherlands, Hungary and Poland. The remainder came from all over the world, with Nigerians, Chinese and Albanians especially prominent.

Catherine Bearder, a Liberal Democrat MEP, said official statistics on this "vile trade" were just the tip of the iceberg. Victims of trafficking come to official attention when they are arrested or escape, she said. "Very, very few are rescued by the authorities and for me that is shocking." Too often, police forces "see the crime, not the person, they see them as illegal immigrants."

The MEP, who spearheaded an anti-trafficking resolution in the European parliament last month, said EU authorities needed to do more to rescue victims and help them recover.

EU law requires countries to provide victims of trafficking with at least 30 days of recovery, including accommodation, medical treatment and legal advice. The UK offers a 45-day "reflection period," when the person cannot be deported.

The MEP would like to see a longer period for recovery. Highlighting the plight of people sold into in sex slavery she said:

"We are much better now at treating people who are raped and give them the protection of the law, but these girls have been raped night after night after night. I think we should be prepared to give them longer support of reflection and more support in rebuilding their lives."

She also urged governments to get to grips with the migration crisis. "When the migrants land on Europe's shores, when they are not properly looked after, they are absolutely ripe victims for the traffickers."

Yvette Cooper, chair of Labour's refugee task force, said the EU played a central role in the fight against human trafficking: "Being in the EU gives our police the tools they need to bring evil human trafficking gangs to justice, including vital cooperation through Europol."

In the past year, 250 suspected human traffickers have been arrested in joint operations supported by Europol, the EU police agency.

Cooper said: "Leaving Europe would be a gift to criminals that would weaken our efforts to stamp out this evil trade."

> "Immigrants may help foreign firms
> find investment opportunities in
> the host country and foster foreign
> direct investment."

Immigration Affects Investment and Productivity in Host and Home Countries

Volker Grossmann

In the following viewpoint, Volker Grossmann examines the effects of immigration on economic components and investment success within the countries that host immigrants. The author considers how the immigration policies of these countries influence the situation. Volker Grossmann is professor of economics at the University of Zurich.

As you read, consider the following questions:

1. Does the viewpoint carry a generally favorable view of immigrants who are investors?
2. Has this subject been studied very often, according to the viewpoint?
3. Are native populations or immigrants more likely to be granted a patent?

M igration policies need to consider how immigration affects investment behavior and productivity, and how these effects vary with the type of migration. College-educated immigrants may do more to stimulate foreign direct investment and research and development than low-skilled immigrants, and productivity effects would be expected to be highest for immigrants in scientific and engineering fields. By raising the demand for housing, immigration also spurs residential investment. However, residential investment is unlikely to expand enough to prevent housing costs from rising, which has implications for income distribution in society.

Immigration by high-skilled workers attracts foreign direct investment, helps firms find investment opportunities abroad, and raises per capita income by boosting productivity. However, despite triggering residential investment in the host country, immigration also raises housing costs, with undesirable income distribution effects. Policymakers should thus consider selective immigration policies that attract high-skilled workers, accompanied by redistributive measures that benefit low-income households in the host country and by compensating measures for the home countries that lose high-skilled migrants.

Motivation

Modern economic growth theory suggests that the interaction of technological progress and capital accumulation is the ultimate source of long-term economic growth. Whether immigration flows cause changes in labor productivity through investments in capital and research and development (R&D) is an important issue for policymakers. Examining how immigration affects capital formation requires a dynamic perspective that includes the effects on the accumulation of intangible assets (knowledge capital) as well as physical assets. For instance, technological improvements could arise as a result of the immigration of high-skilled workers with science and engineering skills. Moreover, immigrants may help foreign firms find investment opportunities in the host country and foster foreign direct investment (FDI).

Also relevant to migration policy are the potentially differential impacts of temporary and permanent immigration. The income distribution effects through the impact on housing costs also need to be considered. If immigration raises the demand for housing faster than supply is able to expand, owners of land and housing property will gain while tenants will be hurt.

Discussion of Pros and Cons

The interaction between international migration and investment has been studied much less than, for example, the labor market effects of immigration on native-born populations and foreign-born workers already living in host countries. In the studies surveyed here, immigrants are typically defined as foreign-born individuals aged 25 or older. Although the shorter-term effects of immigration on employment and wages that have typically been found in the empirical literature are small, migration may lead to large increases in wage income by enhancing FDI in the home and the host countries and productivity in the host country.

Migration and Physical Capital Investment

Measures of FDI flows capture international movements of physical (productive) capital rather than other financial assets. FDI is one potential channel through which migration could affect labor productivity in both home and host regions. That is because immigrants may reduce information frictions that typically lead to a bias by firms against investing in business ventures in foreign countries, about which firms know much less than they do about their home country. Increasing FDI may not only raise the physical capital stock, but also improve technology and thus result in productivity gains.

For a pooled sample of OECD countries, [there is] only a weakly positive (although statistically significant) relationship between net migration flows (defined as total migration inflow minus migration outflow over a five-year period as a share of the average population over the same period) and the sum of net FDI flows over five years as the share of total gross domestic product over the same five years. The net migration rate is lagged by five years (migration data cover the period 1965–2009 and FDI data the period 1970–2014) in order to capture the notion that migration (for example, in the period 1965–1969) affects FDI five years later (in the period 1970–1974).

Inward Foreign Direct Investment

According to theoretical models, under conditions of international or interregional capital mobility, labor market integration that leads to immigration of workers attracts capital inflows because of the complementarity between capital and labor in producing goods and services. Analogously, emigration slows capital formation.

It is important to distinguish the causal effect of migration on capital movements, which is strongly positive, from the correlation between them, which may be weak. Even when the causal effect is positive, labor and capital may move in opposite directions across countries and regions. For that reason, little correlation may be observed between capital accumulation and labor flows, even though the causal effect from net migration to the change in the capital stock is unambiguously positive. A prime example is the opposite movement of labor and capital following reunification of Germany in 1990. Large labor flows moved from East to West Germany, while capital accumulated faster in the East. Neoclassical growth theory suggests that if the integration of labor markets leads to labor outflows from a less developed region with a capital stock per capita that is below its long-term level, capital will also move into the region but at a slower rate than without emigration. If labor market integration occurs when the regions involved are sufficiently developed, labor and capital may flow in the same direction.

The challenge for empirical research is to identify causal effects between immigration and FDI. One study looks at the two-way relationship of stocks of immigrants and stocks of inward FDI from foreign countries into the 16 German states over the period 1991–2002. It finds that inward FDI is significantly increased by a higher stock of immigrants, if it comes from high-income countries. One possible explanation for this effect is that immigrants assist in interactions with foreign companies in their home country, thus helping overcome information problems. It is interesting to note that, unlike a higher stock of immigrants, a larger domestic labor force does not promote inward FDI, so it is not just the larger population size that attracts inward FDI.

Outward Foreign Direct Investment

There is also evidence that a higher stock of immigrants has a positive impact on the stock of international bank loans from the host country to the immigrants' home country. The effect is particularly large when the immigrants are high-skilled and the two countries do not share a common language, legal heritage, or colonial past. This suggests that immigrants are particularly important for facilitating cross-border financial flows when informational problems are severe.

As is the case for bank loans, there may also be a positive effect from immigration on outward FDI from the host country to the immigrants' home country. One study suggests that a larger immigration stock of both low- and high-skilled workers in the US in 1990 led to higher subsequent growth of outward FDI financed by US firms over 1990–2000. The channels through which immigration affects outward FDI may differ for low- and high-skilled migrants, however. One hypothesis is that investors in developed countries with little advance information about the quality of the labor force in developing countries may observe a rather high productivity of immigrants despite their few formal qualifications, take it as signal of the quality of the labor force in the home country of the immigrants, and thus may be more positively inclined to invest there than they would be without that signal. High-skilled immigrants, by contrast, may actively contribute to the creation of international business networks.

Demonstrating causality is usually tackled by predicting migration using variables that affect migration but have no direct effect on investment or productivity gains. Using predicted rather than actual migration avoids that the estimated migration effects actually come from omitted determinants of investment and productivity that are correlated with migration and would therefore bias estimation results. The most common approach to avoiding such omitted-variable bias is to use historically rooted migration stocks of different immigration groups as a predictor of migration. The approach is based on the notion that potential migrants determine where to migrate based on the number of prior migrants from their country, who can ease their migration by providing a social network based on family or cultural ties.

This method is used, for instance, in a study that accounts for the possibility that outward US FDI induces migration of workers in foreign subsidiaries to the US headquarters of multinational companies. The study predicts the total stock of migrants from a home country using the share of the stock of migrants in that country's population 30 years earlier. The results suggest that a 1% increase in the stock of college-educated immigrants in the US raises the stock of outward FDI from the US to the home country of the immigrants by about 0.5%. The effect is slightly lower for an increase in the stock of all immigrants.

Savings and Remittance Behavior of Immigrants

It is also interesting to examine the savings behavior of migrants, to see whether they invest their savings in the host country or remit them to their family members who have not migrated. The literature suggests that both the savings rate and the amount of remittances depend on whether migrants are temporary or permanent. For example, immigrants in Germany seem to have lower saving rates, on average, than native-born residents with similar characteristics. Immigrants who plan to stay only temporarily, however, tend to save more and not less than natives; they remit more than immigrants who plan to stay permanently. Thus, remittances are a major motive for savings, particularly for temporary migrants who plan to return home some time in the future. Those savings are not invested in the host country but may help to accumulate productive capital in the home country. Particularly in home countries where credit markets for financing productive investments are underdeveloped, remittances may be able to boost school enrollment, reduce child labor, and promote entrepreneurship.

Migration and Knowledge Capital Formation

Immigration may also be important for the accumulation of intangible assets. High-skilled immigrants with science, engineering, and other professional skills may contribute to technological improvements in the host countries. While it is common to use formal intellectual property, such as number of patents, to measure innovation, informal innovations in tacit knowledge and organizational improvements can also lead to productivity gains. Thus, to gauge the joint impact of immigration on intangible assets through observable and unobservable R&D, one needs to look not only at the number of patents but also at total factor productivity (the share of output that is not explained by the amount of inputs used in production).

Patent Activity, Innovation, and Productivity

A survey of US college graduates offers evidence on the patenting behavior of immigrants and native-born residents. Immigrant graduates are one percentage point more likely (probability of 1.9%) than native graduates (0.9% probability) to be granted a patent. That difference can be attributed entirely to the fact that the share of immigrants with a science or engineering degree is higher than the share of the native-born population. These results suggest that increasing college-graduate immigrants' share of the population by one percentage point raises the number of patents per capita by 6%.

On the other hand, it has been argued that there could be other reasons for this finding and that a country does not gain from increased patenting through the immigration of scientists and engineers. There may be fears that immigrants' patents will crowd out the patenting activity of native-born workers. It is also possible in this case that if the students had not immigrated to the US, they would have applied for their patents elsewhere and the US might still have benefited from these patents through cross-country knowledge spillovers.

However, the evidence does not support these suggested theoretical possibilities challenging the effect of immigration on patenting. For instance, a study using 1940–2000 US state data points to positive creativity spillovers within the US from a higher share of college-graduate immigrants on the patenting activity of the native-born population. To address the possibility that this finding simply reflects that immigrants choose host countries with high patenting activity, the study looked at changes in patents over time. It predicted the share of immigrants in the workforce (ages 18–65) using the stock of immigrants in 1940 from various home countries. The results suggest that a one percentage point increase in the workforce share of immigrants with a college degree (3.5% in 2000) boosts patents per capita by 13.2% within 10 years. The results are similar over 30-year and 50-year periods. The effects of analogous increases in the college-educated native population over 10, 30, and 50 years are just 2–6%. Moreover, a one percentage point increase in the share of immigrant scientists and engineers in the workforce boosts the number of patents per capita by an astonishing 52%—more than twice as much as for a similar increase in the share of scientists and engineers in the native-born population. Thus, there is a clear boost in patents associated with the immigration of college graduates, particularly the immigration of scientists and engineers.

Overall Productivity Effects

Other studies examine the overall productivity effects of immigration, not just through patenting. Again, the US offers a good opportunity to examine the importance of foreign-born college-educated STEM (science, technology, engineering, and mathematics) workers. The US H-1B visas allow foreign workers to migrate temporarily to the US to work in "specialty" occupations such as those requiring these skills. One study estimates the increase in science and engineering workers attributable to changes in the number of H-1B visas issued in 219 US cities over 1990–2010. The results suggest that a one percentage point increase in the share of foreign-born scientists and engineers in the working population boosts the average weekly wages of native-born college-educated workers by 8–11% and those of native-born non-college-educated workers by almost 4%. These results suggest positive productivity effects. However, the increase in the share of foreign-born scientists and engineers in the working population over the period of the study was just 0.53 percentage points (two-thirds of the total increase in the employment share of such workers in US cities). It is unclear, though, whether the large effects found in this study would hold with heavier inflows of foreign-born science and engineering workers, possibly of lower average quality.

Long-term effects could also come from attracting foreign-born PhD students to scientific and engineering fields. There is evidence that these students increase academic output (as measured

WORK DEFICITS WILL INCREASE MIGRATION WORLDWIDE

Facing the prospect of poor living standards, a large share of the world population tends to look abroad for better life opportunities. The share of the population willing to migrate permanently is highest in Africa and Latin America. In addition, the willingness to migrate is particularly acute among youth: on average youth are more willing to migrate permanently than adults by a magnitude of 10 percentage points. And while there are many factors that drive people's willingness to migrate (e.g. humanitarian reasons, armed conflicts, natural disasters, etc.), labour markets and the search for decent work—central to one's livelihood—clearly plays a central role.

"Migration Is Likely to Intensify in the Future as Decent Work Deficits Remain Widespread," International Labour Organization (ILO).

by number of scientific articles). This kind of basic research may have positive productivity effects, although the effects may take longer to arise than for the immigration of science and engineering workers (rather than PhD students).

Rather than focusing on only one country, other studies use international data on bilateral migration stocks across countries. Bilateral migration data are available for 1990 and 2000 for up to 194 countries. The data set includes information on migrants' education level (e.g. on how many college-educated, working-age immigrants from Greece live in France). One study uses the past emigration stock to predict high-skilled migration rates into OECD countries. The evidence suggests a small, positive effect on the ratio of total factor productivity in the host country to that in the home country. For example, a five percentage point increase (a doubling) in the ratio of college-educated migrants from a migrant-sending country to the college-educated population living in an OECD country raises the ratio of total factor productivity in the home country relative to in the host country by one to two percentage points.

Another approach is to predict a country's share of foreign-born population using bilateral migration flows that are determined by geographic and cultural distance between countries and to use this prediction to estimate the effect of a larger immigration share on per capita income and productivity. The results suggest that a one percentage point increase in the immigration share (which averages 4% for the sample of 181 countries for which the required data were available) raises per capita income by about 6–10%. The effect is driven almost entirely by the increase in total factor productivity; the per capita stock of physical capital is basically unaffected. The productivity effect is attributed to immigration's contribution to innovation activity and the diversity of productive skills. By contrast, openness to trade (the sum of exports and imports as a share of GDP) has no effect on per capita income once the migration share is accounted for. This comparison between migration effects and trade effects illuminates possible biases in studies that estimate the effects of trade expansion on per capita income and do not control for the contribution of immigrants.

Population Diversity

Immigration contributes to the diversity of the population in many ways, and it is important to distinguish among them. The literature has focused largely on the change in the composition of education levels in response to immigration. Diversity can also refer to genetic or cultural diversity. The different forms of diversity may not be strongly correlated, and they may have different effects on economic prosperity in the host country. The literature suggests that the optimal degree of diversity balances the positive complementarities in production between immigrant and native-born workers that arise from the different skills associated with different cultural backgrounds and the increasing costs of communicating in a culturally diverse work environment.

When cultural diversity leads to ethnic fragmentation, the effects of diversity may be predominately negative, especially in developing countries. Meanwhile, birthplace diversity (the probability that two individuals drawn randomly from the population were born in different countries) has been shown to have predominantly positive effects. It is viewed as a good measure of skill complementarities between the immigrant and native-born populations. A country's birthplace diversity is composed of the share of immigrants in the population and the birthplace diversity among those immigrants. Both variables are individually found to have a positive effect on per capita income. The effects are larger for skilled immigrants than for unskilled immigrants. Again, this confirms the expectation that positive productivity effects come from skilled immigrants. The positive effects are particularly strong for patent applications per capita and total factor productivity, two potential drivers of higher per capita income. The results still hold after controlling for measures of ethnic, linguistic, and genetic diversity.

Economic Development Consideration: Brain Drain or Brain Gain?

But what about brain drain and the ethics of depriving other countries of their most productive workers? For migration between developed countries, the effects appear to be moderate. The free movement of labor within the EU may aggravate income differences across member countries, while at the same time generating efficiency gains by letting workers move to the location where they are most productive. Equity concerns call for redistributing the efficiency gains in the host countries through compensating public transfers across EU member states.

The impacts may be more severe for immigration from developing to developed countries. There is evidence that lowering immigration barriers in order to increase the likelihood that skilled workers will be able to emigrate from poor countries with low levels of human capital could stimulate human capital investment in home countries that results in a net brain gain rather than a drain. However, the effects differ across countries, and more countries may lose than gain. Thus, skill-selective immigration policies, while most effective in terms of enabling productivity increases in the host country, are clearly at odds with development goals for some poorer countries. This possibility should be taken into account by developed country policymakers. If skill selection of migrants is preferred over broader liberalization of migration policies that includes non-economic reasons for migration, developed country policymakers should consider possible ways of compensating developing countries. Options include offering study visas for potential immigrant students and fostering technology transfers.

Migration and Residential Investment

Numerous studies suggest that immigration also affects housing costs. At the local level, housing prices may fall if low-income-earning immigrants move into a neighborhood and drive out higher-income earners, who relocate to richer neighborhoods. As this then raises housing prices in those neighborhoods, at a less disaggregated level immigration leads to higher housing prices through an increase in overall demand for housing services. Higher demand for housing also leads to higher investment in residential housing. The important question thus is whether the supply response is large enough to offset the price increases from rising demand, at least in the longer term.

The effect of immigration on housing supply through investment in housing is not nearly as well studied as its effect on housing prices. One exception is an investigation of the effect of regional immigration on residential construction in Spain. By using past immigration to predict current immigration at the regional level, the study accounts for the possibility that immigrants locate in economically booming regions. As Spain's total population grew by 1.5% a year over 2001–2010, with an average annual increase in the immigrant share in the population of about 1.3 percentage points, the number of new housing units grew 1.2–1.5% a year. In other words, a one percentage point increase in the immigrant share in the population led to a roughly 1% increase in residential construction. Half the residential construction boom in Spain can thus be attributed to immigration.

Despite the increase in residential construction, however, housing prices increased by about 2% per year. The explanation for this is straightforward. The combined effect of higher demand and higher supply of housing associated with higher population density determines land prices. The land area available for residential construction can be extended only within naturally determined limits. Consequently, land prices are likely to grow in line with housing demand, thus raising housing costs. Land prices are important from an income distribution point of view because land ownership is often highly concentrated among wealthier individuals and historically determined. An immigration-induced increase in housing demand thus provides windfall gains for landowners, with long-term effects on wealth concentration through familial bequests.

Limitations and Gaps

Though consistent, the evidence that immigration is positively related to capital investment, productivity, and innovation is still rather limited and confined largely to the US. More evidence at the regional level within other countries is also needed on the effects of immigration on FDI and the housing market.

No empirical studies have been conducted so far on the two-way interaction between immigration and residential investment. Intuitively, while immigration triggers housing demand and residential investment, inadequate residential investment because of zoning restrictions can lead to high housing prices that discourage immigration. The wage gains of immigrants in the host country compared with the home country could be nullified by rising housing costs in the host country, thereby further discouraging immigration. It would thus be interesting to know more about the interaction of immigration and zoning and housing construction regulations for residential construction.

The evidence strongly suggests that high-skilled immigrants stimulate capital investment and raise productivity in the host country, but much less is known about the potential effects of migration, particularly of low-skilled migrants, on capital formation in home countries. A potential avenue for such impacts is through remittances, which can, among others, support entrepreneurship among migrants' family members who remain behind in the home country.

Summary and Policy Advice

Empirical evidence suggests that immigration of educated workers attracts FDI, helps firms find investment opportunities abroad, and raises per capita income by enhancing labor productivity. The immigration of scientists and engineers, in particular, stimulates innovation in the host country through new patents. The migration of low-skilled workers seems to have less impact on capital formation in host countries. The evidence supports the design of selective immigration policies to attract high-skilled workers, particularly those with science and engineering skills. Greater birthplace diversity in a population through immigration is also found to foster economic prosperity, particularly if immigrants are well-educated.

However, there is the issue of potential brain drain in developing countries that lose their skilled workforce in response to skill-selective immigration policies in host countries. Such emigration may conflict with development goals and may lead to a net skill loss in home countries. Admitting more students from developing countries on student visas in developed countries may be a way to compensate for brain drain.

From a development policy perspective, the main benefit of emigration for the home country may come from remittances, from both high- and low-skilled migrants. Because remittances tend to be higher from temporary migrants than from permanent migrants, providing opportunities for temporary work in developed countries may be conducive to economic development in home countries. However, temporary migrants have less incentive to learn the host country language, which is an obstacle for improving their earnings prospects over time. This point may be particularly relevant for refugees, who should quickly be moved onto the track of permanent residence in the host country after their refugee status is approved.

Despite the many potentially positive effects of immigration, policymakers have to be aware that high levels of immigration can provoke a backlash against liberal immigration policies in host countries, especially if housing prices rise as a consequence. Clearly, not everyone in the host country benefits from the efficiency gains from immigration. Possible measures to redress the imbalance include transfers to low-income households (who typically rent rather than own housing property), possibly financed by increases in taxation of housing property, wealth, and bequests. Thus any undesirable income distribution effects associated with higher housing prices could be addressed by the tax-transfer system instead of by limiting immigration and forgoing the related positive impacts.

Periodical and Internet Sources Bibliography

The following articles have been selected to supplement the diverse views presented in this chapter.

ACLU, "Human Rights and Immigration," https://www.aclu.org /issues/human-rights/human-rights-and-immigration.

Lauren Alexander, "Immigration as a Social Problem," University of Sunderland Social Sciences Blog, October 7, 2017, https:// sunderlandsocialsciences.wordpress.com/2017/10/07/571/.

European Civil Protection and Humanitarian Aid Operations, "Forced Displacement: Refugees, Asylum Seekers and Internally Displaced People," July 22, 2021, https://ec.europa.eu/echo/what /humanitarian-aid/forced-displacement-refugees-asylum -seekers-and-internally-displaced-people-idps_en.

Claire Felter, Danielle Renish, and Amelia Cheatham, "The U.S. Immigration Debate," Council on Foreign Relations, August 31, 2021, https://www.cfr.org/social-issues/immigration-and -migration.

Robert Kahn, "Push Me, Pull You, Around the World," Courthouse News Service, September 10, 2021, https://www.courthousenews .com/push-me-pull-you-around-the-world.

The New Humanitarian, "Migration: An In-Depth Collection of Global Reporting of Refugees, Asylum Seekers, Migrants, and Internally Displaced People," https://www.thenewhumanitarian .org/migration.

Open Society Foundations, "Why Does the U.S. Need Immigration Reform?" May 2019, https://www.opensocietyfoundations.org /explainers/why-does-us-need-immigration-reform.

Joel Rose, Angela Kocherga, and Max Riulin-Nader, "As More Migrants Arrive, US Expands Efforts to Identify and Address Most Vulnerable," National Public Radio, May 12, 2021, https:// www.npr.org/2021/05/12/995983500/as-more-migrants-arrive-u -s-grants-more-exceptions-to-allow-in-the-most-vulnerab.

What Is the Future of Immigration Policy?

Chapter Preface

The US Congress has rejected large-scale immigration reform repeatedly over the last few decades. These reforms failed due to populist opposition based on xenophobia, with both Democrats and Republicans working together often to defeat bills that would have helped guest workers stay in the country.

These failed policies all would have offered legalization of illegal immigrants now living in the US and a liberalizing of legal permanent immigration and temporary immigration status through an expanded temporary guest worker program for low-skill workers. This comprehensive approach was supposed to "fix" the system by eliminating laws that supposedly create illegal immigration.

New bills do need to address liberalization as the key to immigration reform, but maybe they need to come from different stakeholders. One proposal is for state-based visas that would allow state governments to accept new immigration based on the diversity of immigrants' economic situations. Others have proposed a system where local governments could work with private entities or sponsors to bring refugees to their communities. Both ideas emphasize the engagement of local governments and take the pressure off the federal government.

But this is just one avenue. Grover Norquist offered a proposal that would allow members of Congress to sponsor immigrants for legal permanent residencies. University professor Justin Guest suggests that the federal government begin by collecting much better data on new immigrants and track their outcomes, and Steve Kuhn of IDEAL Immigration has offered an idea whereby visas are sold to employers, providing they have made offers to foreign workers that would match the cost.

These proposals are just a few new ideas that may be incorporated into future legislation as the United States, like the rest of the world, grapples with the immigration crisis.

> *"Migration policies are one of the
> most important, and underused,
> tools to reduce poverty and
> promote development."*

These Countries Have the Best Immigration Policies

Owen Barder and Petra Krylová

In the following viewpoint, Owen Barder and Petra Krylová argue that immigration is an important and underlooked tool in the eradication of poverty worldwide. The authors introduce readers to the Commitment to Development Index. Owen Barder is former director of the Center for Global Development Europe. Petra Krylová is former policy analyst at the Center for Global Development Europe.

As you read, consider the following questions:

1. What is the Commitment to Development Index?
2. What countries are most friendly to students from developing countries?
3. Why do the authors say that attending migration conventions can produce migration-friendly policies?

A s President Obama convenes an important global summit on refugees, and world leaders at the UN General Assembly address the burgeoning issue of migration and forced displacement, we've taken a closer look at how the richest countries in the world support development and the alleviation of poverty through their migration policies. Migration is one of the seven components of our Commitment to Development Index, an annual exercise to marshall millions of data points to track how rich country policies affect the world's poorest people and places, across seven different policy areas.

We will be publishing the full index in October, but we are revealing the CDI's migration rankings now, so they may offer a backdrop for the discussions in New York. Read on to find out how countries measure up.

The Who, What and Why

Migration policies are one of the most important, and underused, tools to reduce poverty and promote development. In the words of our colleague Michael Clemens, we are leaving trillions of dollars on the sidewalk (or pavement). As Clemens has convincingly argued, migration leads to a development gain, not a brain drain. Increased opportunities for well-managed migration bring massive increases in incomes and well-being for individuals, their families and their countries, through higher earnings potential, remittances, trade, and the increased circulation of ideas and knowledge.

To arrive at the index for each country, we look at three broad aspects of rich countries' migration policies. First, their willingness to accept migrants from the developing world; second, how well those migrants are integrated; and third, whether the country participates in a raft of international conventions on migration.

Based on those broad criteria, New Zealand, Norway and Australia have the most development-friendly migration policies; while the Visegrad four—Czech Republic, Hungary, Poland and Slovakia—languish at the bottom of our table of 27 rich countries. Of the G7 major economies, Canada ranks highest for its migration policies, at 4th place, with Germany 6th and Italy at number 12. The US, Japan, UK and France all lie in the bottom half of the table.

More Detail on Where Our Numbers Come From

First we score countries on the number of people they accept: migrants and students from developing countries; and refugees and asylum seekers; and we look at these broadly in proportion to their population. Australia and New Zealand have the largest inflow of immigrants relative to their populations, while, if you've been following news reports of the reaction to (mainly) Syrian refugees arriving in Eastern and Central Europe, you perhaps won't be surprised to learn that the least open are the Visegrad countries—Czech Republic, Hungary, Poland and Slovakia. New Zealand and Australia are also the most welcoming toward students from developing countries. On this measure, the Czech and Slovak Republics again find themselves at the bottom, where they are joined by Denmark and the Netherlands. (To be fair, the relatively low numbers of people wanting to study in these countries may have something to do with the perceived difficulty of the language, as well as how welcoming they are to students.) Though the Netherlands does badly on students, it can boast of rivalling Sweden for being most open to refugees and asylum seekers. Portugal, Slovakia and South Korea accept the fewest refugees, and Japan and Poland accept the least asylum seekers.

The benefits to migrants, and their families and countries of origin, depend not only on numbers but on how those people are treated and the opportunities that are available to them in their new home. We use data from the Migrant Integration Policy Index (MIPEX), a tool which comprehensively assesses whether countries have good policies to support the integration of migrants. MIPEX takes into account 167 policy indicators, which are grouped into 8 categories: education, health, political participation, family reunion, anti-discrimination, access to nationality, and permanent residence. Among the CDI countries, Portugal and Sweden top the list for integrating migrants, followed by Finland, Belgium, and Canada.

Finally, we look at the extent to which countries participate in international conventions on migration. We understand, of course, that international conferences often have only a distant connection to people's real lives; but we also know that over time, international conventions help to establish standards, norms and principles that help shape the behaviour of the international community and individual countries. We argue that there are therefore long-run benefits from countries being willing to agree to these standards, even if they are not always able to live up to their commitments in full immediately. The migration component therefore gives countries credit for ratifying three international agreements: the 1949 Migration for Employment Convention, the 1975 Migrant Workers Convention, and the Protocol to Prevent, Suppress and Punish Trafficking in Persons. Only three countries—Italy, Norway, Portugal—are party to all three conventions, while Japan and South Korea have ratified none of them.

Migration policies reflect the economic, social and political circumstances of each country, and it is foolish to claim that any country could simply adopt the policies being pursued elsewhere. Nonetheless, looking at the fine detail of countries' policies can help us understand where there might be room for improvement, and help us to identify inspiring examples of countries that do this well.

And the CDI migration scores are an element of the annual Commitment to Development Index, along with hundreds of other indicators across six other policy areas: aid, trade, finance, security, climate and technology.

> *"Most past attempts by the federal government to conduct a comprehensive immigration overhaul have failed, either at a Congressional level or at an implementation level."*

There Are Solutions to America's Immigration Problem

Ideal Immigration

In the following viewpoint, Ideal Immigration presents the significant legislation that has shaped immigration policy in the United States. The author begins with an overview of the Immigration Reform and Control Act of 1986 under President Ronald Reagan and ends with a look at current reforms and bills being considered. Ideal Immigration is a Canada-based immigration and naturalization service.

As you read, consider the following questions:

1. What are some of the things that the Immigration Reform and Control Act of 1986 established?
2. What percentage of immigrants are granted entry to the US based on family connections?
3. What is a DREAMer?

"The Past, Present, and Future of Immigration Policy," Ideal Immigration, August 1, 2019. Reprinted by permission.

The question of what to do about immigration in America is not an easy one to answer. While most would agree that the safety of Americans comes first, we encounter more disagreement when the topic of humanity vs. justice comes into question. Many are seeking a moderate solution that upholds the letter of the law, while avoiding isolating America from the rest of the world through aggressive anti-immigration policy.

Several laws and proposals have passed through Congress as the immigration debate continues, but still a consensus has not been reached. Both parties are seeking a bipartisan approach that takes into account the safety and economic security of our country, while still maintaining some level of compassion and tolerance.

The Status of American Immigration Policy

According to Pew Research: "For years, proposals have sought to shift the nation's immigration system away from its current emphasis on family reunification and employment-based migration, and toward a points-based system that prioritizes the admission of immigrants with certain education and employment qualifications."

The shift from family-focus to economy focus is a tough one to make. The majority of legal immigrants entered the country through a family-sponsorship.

In 2017, 66% of all legal immigrants were granted entry based on family connections. Twelve-percent were employment-based immigrants, 11% were refugees, and 5% benefitted from the diversity visa lottery. The Trump administration would reduce the number of family-sponsored immigrants to approximately 33% of all entrants.

Most past attempts by the federal government to conduct a comprehensive immigration overhaul have failed, either at a Congressional level or at an implementation level. Does the solution lie in the Workforce Innovation and Opportunity Act?

Let's take a look at three of the most recent large-scale immigration reform bills: the 1986 Immigration and Reform and Control Act, the Border Security and Immigration Reform

Act of 2018, and the aforementioned Workforce Innovation and Opportunity Act.

Prior to 1986, the last major immigration reform had taken place 11 years prior, with the 1965 Immigration and Nationality Act, which eliminated quotas based on national origin and implemented the familial relationship entry system that we see today.

S. 1200: Immigration Reform and Control Act of 1986

Signed into law on November 6, 1986, by Ronald Reagan, the Immigration Reform and Control Act sought to tighten control at the border, impose fines on employers who knowingly hired unauthorized immigrants, and allow unauthorized immigrants who had lived in the country since 1982 to seek legal status with amnesty. Additionally, it allowed agricultural workers who had worked for at least 90 days to apply for permanent legal residency.

The bill was sponsored by Senator Alan K. Simpson (R-WY) during the 99th Congress. It passed through the Senate with 63% approval. The bill was also called the Simpson-Mazzoli Act and the Reagan Amnesty.

A summary of the bill follows:

- Penalized employers for knowingly hiring or recruiting undocumented immigrants
- Required employers to know and attest to the immigration status of their employees
- Allowed seasonal agricultural workers who had worked more than 90 days to claim legal status and continue their work in the United States
- Legalized all immigrants who had arrived in America before January 1, 1982, so long as they pled guilty to the crime of illegal entry, paid a fine and back taxes, were able to prove that they were innocent of crimes, and that they passed a U.S. history, government, and English test.

This bill attempted to strike the balance between humane treatment of undocumented immigrants already contributing to the American economy and holding them accountable for breaking the law. While it seems like the ideal situation at face value, the numbers showed otherwise.

While the bill set out to stop unauthorized immigration, the number has steadily climbed over the last three decades. In 1986, there were 5 million unauthorized immigrants in the United States. Today, there are over 10.5 million.

Why has growth continued? The *Washington Post* posits that a major contributor was that after amnesty had been claimed by those who could claim it or even knew about the law, everyone expected the other remaining immigrants to just leave. Obviously, that didn't happen.

Additionally, agriculture workers who once worked a "circuit" of farms in California, then went back to Mexico after the growing season, found it safer to remain in America. Crossing back and forth presented more opportunities to be caught, but remaining in Mexico simply wasn't an option—They would be leaving their jobs and homes behind.

H.R. 6136 (115TH): Border Security and Immigration Reform Act of 2018

Sponsored by Virginia Representative Bill Goodlatte, H.R. 6136 was a nearly 300 page long bill that sought to overhaul the current American immigration system in its entirety. It was introduced on June 19, 2018, into the 115th Congress, which ran from January 3, 2017, to January 3, 2019.

This is the most detailed and extensive immigration reform proposal in recent years.

A summary of the bill follows:

Division A—Border Enforcement

- Title I: Border Security
  - Strengthen requirements for barriers along the southern border

- · Department of Homeland Security would be required to "improve physical barriers, tactical infrastructure, and technology to achieve situational awareness and operational control of the border."
- · Deployment of "specific capabilities" to nearly two dozen sectors
- · Requirement for the Commissioner of U.S. Customs and Border Protection to "hire, train, and maintain by 2023 an active duty presence of no fewer than 26,370 full-time agents and 27,725 full-time officers, 1,657 agents for Air and Marine Operations, 300 new K-9 units, 100 horseback officers and 50 horses, an increase of 50 officers for search and rescue operations, an increase of 50 officers focused on tunnel detection and technology, 631 agricultural specialists, no fewer than 550 special agents within the Office of Professional Responsibility, and no fewer than 700 full-time equivalents in the Office of Intelligence.

- Title II: Emergency Port of Entry Personnel and Infrastructure Funding
  - · Construction of new ports of entry on the northern and southern border
  - · One month pilot for license plate readers at the top three busiest entry points
  - · Deployment of non-intrusive passenger vehicle inspection system
  - · Implementation of a "biometric exit data system."
- Title III: Visa Security and Integrity
  - · New fees assessed with visas to pay for visa security programs
  - · Electronic passport biometric screening

- Individuals from "countries determined high risk" would be subjected to social media reviews
- Title IV: Transnational Criminal Organization Illicit Spotter Prevention and Elimination
  - Makes hindering and "spotting" of border and custom controls illegal

Division B—Immigration Reform
- Title I: Lawful Status for Certain Children Arrivals
  - Grants "contingent non-immigrant status to individuals in the Deferred Action for Childhood Arrivals category."
  - Applicants for the program must be under 31, enrolled in an education institute or have a diploma/GED, with no criminal convictions
  - Applicants must pay a $1000 fee in exchange for 6 years of "continent nonimmigrant" status, with additional 6-year terms available
- Title II: Immigrant Visa Allocations and Priorities
  - Eliminates diversity lottery in exchange for 55,000 merit-based visas
  - Eliminates Married Children of U.S. Citizens and Siblings of Adult U.S. Citizens visas in exchanged for employment-based visas
  - Applicants would "garner prioritization" based on:
    - Education level
    - English language proficiency
    - Military service
    - Continuous employment
    - Green cards available at the rate of 78,400 per year
- Title III: Unaccompanied Alien Children; Interior Immigration Enforcement

- Equal treatment of all unaccompanied minors by "ensuring the safe and expeditious return to their home country of children from both contiguous and noncontiguous countries, unless the child has a legitimate asylum claim." These children must not be separated from their parents while in custody
  - Undocumented immigrants who are "dangerous criminals" must stay in detention until they are removed from the US
  - Prevents the entry of gang members and terrorists
- Title IV: Asylum Reform
  - "Combats asylum fraud by increasing the credible fear standard to require a determination that is 'more probable than not' that the asylum seeker's statements are true"
- Title V: USCIS
  - U.S. Citizenship and Immigration Services are exempt from the Paperwork Reduction Act for three years

The bill failed in the House on June 27, 2018, with a vote of 121-301 against.

Why the Bill Failed: Views from the Senate and House

Goodlatte's bill failed with nearly half of Republican voters and all Democrat voters in the House voting against it. Many found that the bill was blatantly partisan.

Representative Jeff Denham (R-CA) told ABC News, "What was obvious today is that Republicans cannot pass a 218 Republican bill, just as Democrats couldn't pass one in 2010… It's important to recognize that it's going to take a bipartisan bill that both addresses border security as well as a permanent fix for Dreamers."

Rep. Carlos Curbelo (R-FL) agreed with his peer. He said, "What we witnessed today was a minority of Republicans joining every Democrat in the House to double down on a failed, broken, inefficient, unfair and at times cruel immigration system. They prefer the petty politics of immigration instead of the solutions for immigration."

Others felt that the bill was unfair to DREAMers, many of whom have lived in the United States since their early childhood. A 2017 *New York Times* article notes that the average DREAMer came to the country when they were 6 years old.

In an article on Medium, Congressman Seth Moulton (D-MA) stated that he voted against the bill because it was a "so-called 'compromise' immigration bill that falls far short of addressing the major challenges facing our nation's immigration system." He also stated, "Seeking asylum is a legal right recognized by the United States and democracies around the world. This legislation would diminish protections for those seeking asylum by raising the "credible fear" test, which is used by Immigration Judges to determine if an individual has a legitimate fear of persecution or death."

Both Republicans and Democrats are seeking a less extreme option, one that modernizes and reworks the shaky foundation that the Immigration Reform and Control Act of 1986 built.

Workforce Visa Act

The Workforce Visa Act is a new employer-chosen visa program that works to enrich the economy, welcome new immigrants, and allow visa holders to become a United States citizen.

It is built on seven planks:

- 1-year guest worker visa, wherein foreign nationals with a valid offer of employment may pay a $2,500 fee to obtain a 1-year guest worker visa. The visa is renewable with another valid offer of employment and $2,500 fee. Employers must follow all relevant labor laws as per their jurisdiction including minimum wage.
- Employers can hire these workers if they pay them back the $2,500 over the 1 year as a part of their monthly wage. Thus, they are incentivized to look for Americans first

because Americans are free and workforce visa holders are incentivized to stay with their original employer to get reimbursed.

- The $2,500 goes into a trust fund for workforce development in the State where the visa holder is employed. The state in which the workforce visa holder is employed will have access to $2,500 of the Workforce Trust Fund. This will be used to fund apprenticeships, job training, job placement, and other workforce development skills.
- Visa holders may adjust status to legal permanent residence after 10 consecutive years if they pay an additional $25,000 or work an additional 10 years. This is an incentive to comply with the law. Current visa paths towards legal permanent resident are confusing, hard to access, or do not exist. By clear path, it incentivizes foreign workers to comply with the law, work hard, and be rewarded instead of overstaying their visa.
- Visa holders are not eligible for any means tested public benefits of any kind and if they adjust status to legal permanent resident, they cannot claim benefits retroactively.
- All employers who hire these visa-holding employees must be a part of E-Verify.
- All visa holders will have the right to join a labor union if it exists at their place of work.

The Workforce Visa Act would solve several issues that we are facing with our current immigration policy. First, we would be able to prevent the impending social security crisis.

From Vox: "Undocumented immigrants and immigrants with legal status pay billions of dollars each year into the Social Security system through payroll taxes. Based on estimates in the trustees report, the more immigrants that come in, the longer the Social Security system will stay solvent. That's because immigrants, on average, are a lot younger than the overall US population, so their retirement is far off. And undocumented immigrants pay for Social Security, but they're not allowed to get benefits."

Additionally, it would work to fund training for Americans and immigrants alike. With the Workforce Trust Fund, people across the United States would have better access to job training programs, job placements, and apprenticeships. Doing so would also boost the prevalence of skill-based trades, many of which are losing traction in a world that increasingly favors technology-based fields.

It would also allow border enforcement to focus more on criminal aliens involved in violent crimes, trafficking, and the narcotics trade, allowing hard-working legal immigrants to continue working in the United States without the temptation to overstay their visa.

While no immigration policy will ever solve every problem, there are solutions that promote our economy, protect families at the border, and place more emphasis on preventing the entrance of violent criminals. The security of Americans and the continued prosperity of our economic system stand to benefit from an act that stays away from reducing legitimate immigration, but instead puts the emphasis on making the process easier for those legally seeking the American dream.

VIEWPOINT 3

> *"Immigrants are accused of stealing jobs from local workers, especially low skilled workers; depriving the local population of social services; and, generally, act as a drag on the economy."*

Anti-Immigrant Movements Have Gained Traction Worldwide

Daud Khan and Leila Yasmine Khan

In the following viewpoint, Daud Khan and Leila Yasmine Khan examine the often politically pushed idea that new immigrants are bad for host countries and are taking native citizens' jobs. The authors argue that the recent push toward this line of thinking is a smoke screen to detract from areas of real concern. Daud Khan is a former United Nations official and is consultant and adviser for various governments and international agencies. Leila Yasmine Khan is an editor and writer based in the Netherlands.

As you read, consider the following questions:

1. What is the real reason the idea of a "clash of cultures" is being pushed in regard to immigration, according to the authors?
2. What is Brexit?
3. Who do the authors say are particularly at risk given the current political climate?

"Clash of Cultures—Is It Real or a Smokescreen?" by Daud Khan and Leila Yasmine Khan, Inter Press Service, April 8, 2021. Reprinted by permission.

The notion of "Clash of Cultures" is most frequently used as a justification for anti-immigrant prejudice and, particularly in Europe and in the USA, for Islamophobia. The reasoning goes as follows: immigrants, especially Muslims, have a deeply different culture from the hosting communities and these differences create unsurmountable tensions and conflicts.

Moreover, immigrants are accused of stealing jobs from local workers, especially low skilled workers; depriving the local population of social services; and, generally, act as a drag on the economy. The only real solution is to stop, or drastically reduce immigration—particularly what is called economic migration—and, if possible, start expelling immigrants that are already there.

Culture is a mix of norms, modes, conventions, beliefs and ideologies. There are major differences in culture between regions and countries; even neighbouring towns or villages may have very different ways of living joyful and sad experiences, such as marriage and deaths, or addressing issues and conflicts.

And there are frictions and irritations when people of different cultures live with each other. These frictions, if poorly handled, can explode into arguments, fights and even riots.

But over the past decade anti-immigrant views, and the cultural stereotyping on which it is based, has been elevated to the primary narrative in many political contexts. In the USA, President Trump made the campaign to "stop the rapists and murderers from Mexico" a signature issue and successfully drew in millions of voters.

In the UK it was a key factor in the Brexit vote. In Europe, the birthplace of democracy and liberalism, anti-immigrant movements are taking "hate-politics" to new heights—immigrants are blamed for crime, disease, scrounging state benefits and unemployment.

The success of anti-immigrant movements among voters has shifted the political balance and made even the traditional mainstream political parties hesitant to appear soft on immigrants.

Even Nobel Prize winner Aung San Suu Kyi fell into the trap of seeing action against aliens and intruders as justified. She stood by silently while the Myanmar army and vigilante Buddhist monks—often considered as icons of peace and solidarity— committed atrocities against Rohingya Muslims who have been living in Myanmar for several generations, arguing that they were illegally in Myanmar and that their ways polluted the purity of the country.

It is an interesting question to speculate why the anti-immigrant movement has become so important; particularly as the consensus among analysts is that immigration is generally beneficial for immigrants, as well as for the countries they emigrate from and for the countries they immigrate to.

For those who emigrate, the benefits are clear. Emigration allows them to substantially increase their incomes often several-fold.

It usually also benefits their families and communities as the money they send home triggers higher investments in both physical and human capital. Generally, their countries of origin also benefit due to higher remittance, and due to the skills that they bring back should they return.

Immigration also benefits the host countries. It provides labour for the hardest and most arduous tasks, for example in agriculture and livestock; for the care of the elderly or of young children; or in running small businesses that require long hours for only low returns, such as neighbourhood convenience stores.

This keeps some of these essential services cheap and also releases natives to engage in more productive activities. In many countries immigrants are also net contributors to the tax system, paying significantly more than they draw in benefits, though the extent of this depends on factors such as the fiscal and benefits regimes in these countries, as well as the age profile, skills set and employment status of immigrants.

Immigration also brings in specific skills that may be limited in the host country. This can range from doctors and health care

THE TOP TEN COUNTRIES TO ACCEPT MIGRANTS

Immigration has roiled politics in countries around the world, as people flee violence, persecution and poverty to seek a better life.

European Union officials are debating future policies because of the Taliban takeover of Afghanistan that has already produced a new wave of Afghans leaving the country.

Mexico's president is urging U.S. officials to invest in Central American nations as a way to slow the migration to the U.S. border.

While there is no universally accepted definition for migrant, the U.N. defines a migrant as being a person who lacks citizenship in her or his host country.

Migration flows stabilized in 2018 and 2019, and then decreased dramatically in 2020, due to the COVID-19 pandemic, according to the most recent OECD report.

Here is a look at the 10 OECD member countries that accepted the most migrants—which includes foreign nationals moving to the country as well as those already there on a permanent basis.

The most recent data for all OECD member countries is from 2018.

1. Germany
2. United States
3. Spain
4. Japan
5. South Korea
6. United Kingdom
7. Turkey
8. Chile
9. Canada
10. Italy

"10 Countries That Take the Most Migrants," U.S. News & World Report L.P., August 24, 2021."

workers, to highly technical know-how in ICT. In the UK and the USA, second generation immigrants are supplying the mainstream political parties with leadership and strategic thinking—clear indication that the host nations are in short supply of these rather vital skills.

But are there negative side effects? Does immigration cause harm, at least to some sections of the population, in the developed host countries? In particular, do they displace local unskilled workers and drive down their wages?

There is decades of empirical research that show the negative side effects of migration are exaggerated. In particular the negative impacts of immigration on the wages of low-skilled native workers in developed countries are relatively small and short-lived.

In the UK, unrestricted immigration from low income EU countries in Eastern Europe more than tripled and the foreign born component of the workforce increased to about 7%. Instead of creating unemployment among low wage British workers, this influx has been accompanied by an expansion of jobs for locals.

Similarly getting rid, or reducing use, of low cost immigrants does little for jobs and incomes of low-skilled domestic workers. When the USA restricted use of seasonal migrant labour in agriculture, instead of hiring native workers, farmers reduced the number of employees by switching crops or investing in new, albeit more expensive technology.

So why has immigration become such an important issue with so much misinformation? One major reason is that it provides a smoke screen for other divisive changes in society, the most important of which is rising inequality.

Over the past three or four decades the world has rapidly become more globalised and interlinked. At the same time technology has drastically changed the employment landscape.

Overall productivity and incomes have increased and most people have seen living standards rise while extreme poverty had declined. But the gains have not been evenly distributed. Some people have done exceedingly well but there have many losers—people who have lost their jobs or seen their incomes drop.

Particularly at risk are young people, especially those with limited skills and education, who have little prospect for a secure and stable job that would allow them to plan a future for themselves and their families.

These changes have created enormous social stresses and strains. Populist parties and populist leaders have been quick to exploit these feelings of unease and difficulty, and immigrants are an easy target to blame.

In fact they are so easy to blame that you actually don't really need any. In the UK many of the Brexit voters came from areas where there are few immigrants but that were hard hit by deindustrialization.

In mainland Europe the most virulent and successful anti-immigrant rhetoric is in countries such as Poland and Hungary, despite the fact that immigrant flows are extremely small.

In the coming decades immigration will remain essential to both Europe and North America. Given their low birth rates, which is being driven down further by the COVID-19 pandemic, immigrants are needed to operate their farms and factories, maintain their living standards and, most importantly, to fund the pensions and health care for their aging populations.

It is therefore incumbent on responsible political parties in the development countries, as well as on intellectuals in both sides of the developing/developed country divide, to counter the toxic narrative on immigration, culture and conflict.

At the same time, the governments of developing countries need to be more forceful and articulate in their defence of rights and treatment of immigrant communities.

And maybe it is time to go even further. Maybe it is time for the developing countries, especially countries from which large numbers of immigrants come—such as Bangladesh, India, Pakistan, Philippines and Romania—to ask to be reimbursed for the costs incurred for educating and caring for the immigrants before they departed.

These countries should request that a part of the taxes their immigrant workers pay should be remitted to their country of origin. And if there are concerns about how the host governments would use these funds, they could be earmarked for certain activities such as health and education. Maybe even agencies such as the World Bank or the UN could offer to manage these funds.

> "The smaller the country, the
> higher its probable proportion of
> foreign-born residents."

Immigration Data Requires Close Interpretation

Gilles Pison

In the following viewpoint, Gilles Pison examines immigration through statistics and interprets the data. The author argues that percentages may tell another story while actual numbers lie as far as immigration problems or concerns. In addition, nations rarely track data on migrant departures, even though these people may be contributing to their former country's economy by sending money back to family. Gilles Pison is an anthropologist and demographer and professor at France's National Museum of Natural History.

As you read, consider the following questions:

1. According to the viewpoint, are immigrants actually a very large group?
2. Why are the numbers of immigrants hard to establish?
3. In 2015, what was the home country of the largest group of immigrants?

"Which Countries Have the Most Immigrants?" by Gilles Pison, The Conversation, March 11, 2019. https://theconversation.com/which-countries-have-the-most -immigrants-113074. Licensed under CC BY-ND-4.0.

The proportion of immigrants varies considerably from one country to another. In some, it exceeds half the population, while in others it is below 0.1%. Which countries have the most immigrants? Where do they come from? How are they distributed across the world? We provide here an overview of the number and share of immigrants in different countries around the world.

According to the United Nations, the United States has the highest number of immigrants (foreign-born individuals), with 48 million in 2015, five times more than in Saudi Arabia (11 million) and six times more than in Canada (7.6 million). However, in proportion to their population size, these two countries have significantly more immigrants: 34% and 21%, respectively, versus 15% in the United States.

Looking at the ratio of immigrants to the total population, countries with a high proportion of immigrants can be divided into five groups:

- The first group comprises countries that are sparsely populated but have abundant oil resources, where immigrants sometimes outnumber the native-born population. In 2015, the world's highest proportions of immigrants were found in this group: United Arab Emirates (87%), Kuwait (73%), Qatar (68%), Saudi Arabia, Bahrain, and Oman, where the proportion ranges from 34% to 51%. The second group consists of very small territories, microstates, often with special tax rules: Macao (57%), Monaco (55%), and Singapore (46%).
- The third group is made up of nations formerly designated as "new countries," which cover vast territories but are still sparsely populated: Australia (28%) and Canada (21%).
- The fourth group, which is similar to the third in terms of mode of development, is that of Western industrial democracies, in which the proportion of immigrants generally ranges from 9% to 17%: Austria (17%), Sweden (16%), United States (15%), United Kingdom (13%), Spain (13%), Germany (12%), France (12%), the Netherlands (12%), Belgium (11%), and Italy (10%).

• The fifth group includes the so-called "countries of first asylum," which receive massive flows of refugees due to conflicts in a neighbouring country. For example, at the end of 2015, more than one million Syrian and Iraqi refugees were living in Lebanon, representing the equivalent of 20% of its population, and around 400,000 refugees from Sudan were living in Chad (3% of its population).

Small Countries Have Higher Proportions of Immigrants

With 29% immigrants, Switzerland is ahead of the United States, while the proportion in Luxembourg is even higher (46%). Both the attractiveness and size of the country play a role. The smaller the country, the higher its probable proportion of foreign-born residents. Conversely, the larger the country, the smaller this proportion is likely to be. In 2015, India had 0.4% of immigrants and China 0.07%.

However, if each Chinese province were an independent country—a dozen provinces have more than 50 million inhabitants, and three of them (Guangdong, Shandong, and Henan) have about 100 million—the proportion of immigrants would be much higher, given that migration from province to province, which has increased in scale over recent years, would be counted as international and not internal migration. Conversely, if the European Union formed a single country, the share of immigrants would decrease considerably, since citizens of one EU country living in another would no longer be counted. The relative scale of the two types of migration—internal and international—is thus strongly linked to the way the territory is divided into separate nations.

The Number of Emigrants Is Difficult to Measure

All immigrants (in-migrants) are also emigrants (out-migrants) from their home countries. Yet the information available for counting emigrants at the level of a particular country is often of poorer quality than for the immigrants, even though, at the global level, they represent the same set of people. Countries are probably less concerned about counting their emigrants than their immigrants, given that the former, unlike the latter, are no longer residents and do not use government-funded public services or infrastructure.

However, emigrants often contribute substantially to the economy of their home countries by sending back money and in some cases, they still have the right to vote, which is a good reason for sending countries to track their emigrant population more effectively. The statistical sources are another reason for the poor quality of data on emigrants. Migrant arrivals are better recorded than departures, and the number of emigrants is often estimated based on immigrant statistics in the different host countries.

The number of emigrants varies considerably from one country to another. India headed the list in 2015, with nearly 16 million people born in the country but living in another; Mexico comes in second with more than 12 million emigrants living mainly in the United States.

Proportionally, Bosnia and Herzegovina holds a record: there is one Bosnian living abroad for two living in the country, which means that one-third of the people born in Bosnia and Herzegovina have emigrated. Albania is in a similar situation, as well as Cape Verde, an insular country with few natural resources.

Some countries are both immigration and emigration countries. This is the case of the United Kingdom, which had 8.4 million immigrants and 4.7 million emigrants in 2015. The United States has a considerable number of expatriates (2.9 million in 2015), but this is 17 times less in comparison to the number of immigrants (48 million at the same date).

Until recently, some countries have been relatively closed to migration, both inward and outward. This is the case for Japan, which has few immigrants (only 1.7% of its population in 2015) and few emigrants (0.6%).

Immigrants: Less Than 4% of the World Population

According to the United Nations, there were 258 million immigrants in 2017, representing only a small minority of the world population (3.4%); the vast majority of people live in their country of birth. The proportion of immigrants has only slightly increased over recent decades (30 years ago, in 1990, it was 2.9%, and 55 years ago, in 1965, it was 2.3%). It has probably changed only slightly in 100 years.

But the distribution of immigrants is different than it was a century ago. One change is, in the words of Alfred Sauvy, the "reversal of migratory flows" between North and South, with a considerable share of international migrants now coming from Southern countries.

Today, migrants can be divided into three groups of practically equal size: migrants born in the South who live in the North (89 million in 2017, according to the United Nations); South-South migrants (97 million), who have migrated from one Southern country to another; and North-North migrants (57 million). The fourth group—those born in the North and who have migrated to the South—was dominant a century ago but is numerically much smaller today (14 million). Despite their large scale, especially in Europe, migrant flows generated since 2015 by conflicts in the Middle East have not significantly changed the global picture of international migration.

Periodical and Internet Sources Bibliography

The following articles have been selected to supplement the diverse views presented in this chapter.

Geoffrey S. Corn and Alyssa N. Shallenberger, "Fixing the Immigration Crisis: The Decisive Point," The Hill, April 6, 2021, https://thehill.com/opinion/immigration/546235-fixing-the -immigration-crisis-the-decisive-point.

European Commission, "Potential Implications of Increasing Significance of Migration," https://knowledge4policy.ec.europa .eu/foresight/topic/increasing-significance-migration/more -potential-implications-relevant-migration_en.

International Rescue Committee, "Refugee Crisis," https://www .rescue.org/topic/refugee-crisis.

Migration Data Portal, "Future Migration Trends," October 20, 2020, https://www.migrationdataportal.org/themes/future-migration -trends.

Babusi Nyoni, "How Artificial Intelligence Can Be Used to Predict Africa's Next Migration Crisis," UNHCR.org, February 10, 2017.

Dan Restrepo, Joel Martinez, and Trevor Sutton, "Getting Migration in the Americas Right," Center for American Progress, June 24, 2019, https://www.americanprogress.org/article/getting -migration-americas-right/.

Karol Suarez, "Cartels Reap Growing Profits in the Smuggling of Migrants Across the US-Mexico Border," *Courier Journal*, July 1, 2021, https://www.courier-journal.com/story/news /investigations/2021/07/01/mexican-cartels-fuel-immigration -crisis-at-us-border/5290082001/.

Amali Tower, "US Border Crisis Is Born of Failed Climate and Migration Policies," Aljazeera, September 15, 2021.

Urban Institute, "Understanding the Consequences of Immigration Policy," https://www.urban.org/features/understanding -consequences-immigration-policy.

Laura Zafrini, "Europe and the Refugee Crisis: The Challenge to Our Civilization," UN, September 19, 2021.

For Further Discussion

Chapter 1
1. Why are definitions important when discussing immigration? Why does language matter when we discuss immigrants?
2. Why is America considered a nation of immigrants? Is that still the case?
3. Define the idea and importance of the "push/pull" model of immigration.

Chapter 2
1. What extended problems does the "crisis of immigration" entail?
2. Is the immigration crisis a US-centric problem? Why or why not?
3. How would your life be different if you were from a family of undocumented immigrants?

Chapter 3
1. Is leaving a minor unattended at a country's border unethical? Why or why not?
2. How does immigration affect a country's economy?
3. Historically, how has US policy toward immigrants changed?

Chapter 4
1. Name a few ideas about how immigration should or could be handled in the future.
2. Identify a personal account from this resource that you felt had special significance to you.
3. How has the COVID-19 pandemic changed immigration issues?

Organizations to Contact

The editors have compiled the following list of organizations concerned with the issues debated in this book. The descriptions are derived from materials provided by the organizations. All have publications or information available for interested readers. The list was compiled on the date of publication of the present volume; the information provided here may change. Be aware that many organizations take several weeks or longer to respond to inquiries, so allow as much time as possible.

American Civil Liberties Union

125 Broad Street
18th Floor
New York, NY 10004
(212) 549-2500
email: aclupreferences@aclu.org
website: www.aclu.org

The ACLU was founded in 1920 in New York City and provides legal services in cases where civil liberties are at risk and supports human rights issues.

American Immigration Council

1331 G Street NW
Suite 200
Washington, DC 20005
website: www.americanimmigrationcouncil.org

The American Immigration Council works to advance positive public attitudes and create a more welcoming America through serving individuals in detention centers, working through the courts to promote fairness, and educating the public. The nonprofit was founded in 1987.

Center for Migration Studies of New York

307 East 60th Street
4th Floor
New York, NY 10022
(212) 337-3080
website: www.cmsny.org

CMS is an educational, nonpartisan think tank based in New York City and is dedicated to domestic and international policy issues, protecting the rights of immigrants worldwide. It was founded in 1964.

Migration Policy Institute

1275 K Street NW
Suite 800
Washington, DC 20005
(202) 266-1940
email: info@migrationpolicy.org
website: www.migrationpolicy.org

This nonpartisan agency is dedicated to improving immigration and integration policies through research and analysis. It was founded in 2001.

National Immigration Forum

10 G Street NE
Suite 500
Washington, DC 20002
(202) 347-0040
website: www.immigrationforum.org

Founded in 1982, the National Immigration Forum focuses on the value immigrants have to America using communications and policy expertise to advocate for more refugees and immigrants.

National Immigration Law Center

3450 Wilshire Boulevard
#108-62
Los Angeles, CA 90010
(213) 639-3900
email: reply@nilc.org
website: www.nilc.org

NILC is a leading US organization in the defense of immigrants of low income in the US. It was founded in 1979 and is based in Los Angeles, California.

New American Economy

c/o Gellar and Company
909 Third Avenue
New York, NY 10022
email: info@newamericaneconomy.org
website: www.newamericaneconomy.org

Founded in 2010, New American Economy is a bipartisan research organization advocating for positive federal, state, and local immigration policies to build the economy and create jobs for all Americans, with emphasis on immigrants.

United Nations High Commissioner for Refugees (UNHCR)

Case Postale 2500
CH-1211 Genève 2 Dépôt
Switzerland
website: www.unhcr.org

The main purpose of the UNHCR is to safeguard the rights and well-being of refugees and immigrant groups. It was begun as part of the 1951 Convention and 1967 Refugee Convention Protocol following World War II.

Upwardly Global

47 Kearny Street, Suite 80
San Francisco, CA 94108
(415) 834-9901
website: www.upwardlyglobal.org

Upwardly Global was established in 1999, the first nonprofit organization to focus on immigrant workforce inclusion. It has offices in four locations in the United States.

US Committee for Refugees and Immigrants

2231 Crystal Drive, Suite 350
Arlington, VA 22202
(703) 310-1130
email: uscri@uscridc.org
website: www.refugees.org

Started in 1911, this organization protects the rights and addresses the needs of persons in forced voluntary migration worldwide and supports their transition to a dignified life. It is based in Arlington, Virginia.

US Immigration and Customs Enforcement (ICE)

PO Box 14475
Pennsylvania Avenue NW
Washington, DC 20044
(866) 347-2423
email: joint.intake@dhs.gov
website: www.ice.gov

ICE is the United States federal law enforcement agency governing immigration issues under the US Department of Homeland Security. It was founded in 2003.

Bibliography of Books

Carolina Bejarano, et al. *Decolonizing Ethnography: Undocumented Immigrants and New Directions in Social Science.* Durham, NC: Duke University Press, 2019.

Ian Goldin. *Exceptional People: How Migration Shaped Our World and Will Define Our Future.* Princeton, NJ: Princeton University Press, 2012.

Adam Goodman. *The Deportation Machine: America's Long History of Expelling Immigrants* (Politics and Society in Modern America). Princeton, NJ: Princeton University Press, 2020.

Rebecca Hamlin. *Crossing: How We Behave and React to People on the Move.* Stanford, CA: Stanford University Press, 2021.

Reece Jones. *White Borders: The History of Race and Immigration in the United States from Chinese Exclusion to the Border Wall.* Boston, MA: Beacon Press, 2021.

Michael LeMay. *Immigration Reform: A Reference Handbook.* Santa Barbara, CA: ABC-CLIO, 2019.

Michael LeMay. *The U.S. Mexico Border: A Reference Handbook.* Santa Barbara, CA: ABC-CLIO, 2022.

William P. Lopez. *Separated.* Baltimore, MD: John Hopkins University Press, 2019.

Ana Raquel Minian. *Undocumented Lives: The Untold Story of Mexican Migration.* Cambridge, MA: Harvard University Press, 2020.

David Nasaw. *The Last Million: Europe's Displaced Persons from World War to Cold War.* London, UK: Penguin, 2021.

Walter J. Nichols. *The Immigrant Rights Movement.* Stanford, CA: Stanford University Press, 2019.

Matt C. Pinsker. *Crisis on the Border: An Eyewitness Account of Illegal Aliens, Violent Crime and Cartels.* Washington, DC: Regenery, 2020.

J. C. Salyer. *Count of Injustice: Law Without Recognition in U.S. Immigration.* Stanford, CA: Stanford University Press, 2020.

Patrice Vecchione and Alyssa Raymond, eds. *Ink Knows No Borders: Poems of the Immigrant and Refugee Experience.* Salem, OR: Triangle Square, 2019.

Harsha Walia. *Border and Rule: Global Migration, Capitalism and the Rise of Racist Nationalism.* Chicago, IL: Haymarket Books, 2021.

Jia Lynn Yang. *One Mighty and Irresistible Tide: The Epic Struggle over American Immigration, 1924–1965.* New York, NY: W. W. Norton, 2021.

Matthew Yglesias. *One Billion Americans: The Case for Thinking Bigger.* New York, NY: Portfolio, 2020.

John Zmirak. *The Politically Incorrect Guide to Immigration.* Washington, DC: Regnery, 2018.

Index

Office of Refugee Resettlement, 46–47, 48

Oman, 158

Operation Border Resolve, 24

P

Pakistan, 87, 88, 90, 93, 94, 95, 98, 155

Papua New Guinea, 95

patents, aquisition of, 41, 124–125

Philippines, 85, 86, 87, 88, 89–90, 93, 94, 95, 155

Pison, Gilles, 157–161

Poland, 116, 137, 138, 155

Portugal, 138, 139

Protocol Relating to the Status of Refugees (1967), 76

push-pull dynamic of immigration, 14, 15, 18, 22–23, 87

Q

Qatar, 158

R

Raftery, Adrian, 26–29

Rankin, Jennifer, 113–117

Reagan, Ronald, 140, 142

Real ID Act of 2005, 57

Refugee Act of 1980, 76, 78

Reichlin-Melnick, Aaron, 61–62, 67

Riggs, Chris, 61

Rohingyas, 90, 93, 94, 100, 101, 104, 152

Romania, 116, 155

S

Samoa, 94, 95, 96

Saudi Arabia, 91, 158

Sauvy, Alfred, 161

Scott, Rick, 60

Selee, Andrew, 52

Shambaugh, Jay, 30–44

Shilhav, Raphael, 55

Simpson, Alan K., 142

Singapore, 85, 86, 158

Slovakia, 137, 138

Solomon Islands, 95

Song, Jay, 82–105

South Korea, 85, 86, 87, 88, 89, 90, 96, 98, 99, 104, 107, 138, 139, 153

Spain, 130, 153, 158

Sri Lanka, 85, 86, 88, 93, 94

Steller, Tim, 59–68

Sweden, 114, 138, 158

Syria, 88, 90, 138, 159

T

Taiwan, 85, 86, 89

Tallon, Emma, 19–25

Texas Band of Kickapoo Act of 1983, 57–58

Thailand, 85, 86, 87, 88, 90, 91, 92–93, 94, 96, 98, 99, 104

Tonga, 95, 96

Treaty of Guadalupe Hidalgo, 54

Trump, Donald/Trump administration, 18, 19, 22–25, 54, 63, 64, 67, 68, 70, 75, 77, 78, 107, 141, 151

Praise for *Worst. President. Ever.*

"An engrossing and seamless combination of the personal and the political, history and lively connections to contemporary politics. . . . with charm, good humor and deep scholarship."

—*Chicago Tribune*

"An excellent history about James Buchanan, placing the 15th president in context . . . extensive research, persuasive arguments to back up the claim and lively writing to keep readers going. . . . This is one of those wonderful books where you're constantly learning, or perhaps, re-learning history."

—*The Star-Ledger* (New Jersey)

"One of [the] books on White House decision-making and crisis management that I'd encourage Trump to read. . . ."

—Carlos Lozada, *Washington Post*

"Strauss digs deep into the life and times of a man whose record of influential incompetence will be tough for any chief executive to ever beat."

—*The Christian Science Monitor*

"Robert Strauss' enjoyable page-turner, *Worst. President. Ever.*, makes the case that James Buchanan, our 15th president, who served from 1857 to 1861, was the worst commander in chief."

—*Atlanta Jewish Times*

"Strauss adroitly and effectively makes his case.... Buchanan, who presided ineffectively over a country that went to war with itself, was indeed the worst."

—*The Virginian-Pilot*

"Part-biography, part travelogue, part meditation on what makes a truly terrible president, Strauss explores the failed one-term presidency of Buchanan.... The discussion of just what we can learn from failed presidencies is illuminating.... For all these reasons and more, put down that Washington biography and give *Worst. President. Ever.* a read."

—*WPSU, Penn State*

"Entertaining study of 'the first plodding-to-the-top president,' a man mercifully forgotten by history. . . . Strauss makes a firm argument for the essential doofusness of the 15th president."

—*Kirkus Reviews*

"Strauss maintains a light tone, but doesn't sacrifice substance in offering solid historical detail and insights into American politics as the country careened toward Civil War."

—*Publishers Weekly*

"One might put forth other candidates for the crown Mr. Strauss has bestowed on Mr. Buchanan, but one cannot dispute the élan with which he makes his case. This is history writing at it should be, but too often isn't: authoritative, yet lively and fun to read."

—David M. Friedman, author of
Wilde in America, *The Immortalists*, and *A Mind of Its Own*

"Authors who want to teach us the secrets of the best are a dime a dozen. Only Robert Strauss could show us what we have to learn from the worst. *Worst. President. Ever.* is a tour de force—entertaining and edifying in equal measure."

—Kermit Roosevelt, author, legal scholar, and
Professor of Law at the University of Pennsylvania

"If you despised W., if Obama fills you with loathing, if you fear apocalyptic consequences with the election of Hillary or Trump . . . then Robert Strauss is here with historical reassurance. A century and a half ago, America survived (just barely) a truly terrible president: a bungler of a politician who did next to nothing as the Union broke apart over slavery."

—David Kinney, author of *The Devil's Diary:
Alfred Rosenberg and the Stolen Secrets of the Third Reich*

"President Buchanan had a great résumé, but in war, peace, race, religion, leadership, friendship, love, and honor he left much to be desired. Strauss weaves the history of this failed president with countless facts and observations about American presidents and his own lifelong fascination with the successes, failures, and foibles of our elected leaders."

—Rush D. Holt, former congressman, Chief Executive Officer of the
American Association for the Advancement of Science

"Strauss makes his case in a manner to be appreciated by both serious historians and modern day politicos. This treatment of a critical piece of Pre-Civil War history will leave readers engaged, entertained, and better equipped to justify their next ranking of Buchanan's true place in American history."

—Michael Smerconish, television and radio host, and
New York Times bestselling author

"A revealing look at President Buchanan and our fascination with ranking those who have been our Commander in Chief."

—Julian Zelizer, author of *The Fierce Urgency of Now:
Lyndon Johnson, Congress and the Battle for the Great Society*

"In a world obsessed with celebrating successes, we can often learn more from studying failure. There's nowhere better to start than James Buchanan, the president who doomed America to a Civil War. This entertaining, informative book is full of lessons for leaders in every office."

—Adam Grant, *New York Times* bestselling author of *Originals* and *Give and Take*

"Robert Strauss has penned a fascinating biography of James Buchanan. With humor and candor, he plumbs the depths of presidential ineptitude while offering compelling sidebars into the history (and vagaries) of presidential rankings and the lives of Buchanan's fellow Bad Presidents."

—Matthew Algeo, author of *Harry Truman's Excellent Adventure:
The True Story of a Great American Road Trip*